MAN'S FIRST LOVE

by Ralph W. Sockman

MAN'S
FIRST
LOVE

THE GREAT COMMANDMENT

Ralph W. Sockman

DOUBLEDAY & COMPANY, INC.

GARDEN CITY, NEW YORK

241
5678m

Library of Congress Catalog Card Number 58–7370

To JULIE,
who knows what love is but cannot yet say the word.

ACKNOWLEDGEMENTS

I am deeply grateful to Marian M. Marcy, Beatrice Meylan, Helen Stanbury, and Geneva Helm for secretarial help in preparing this manuscript; to Mrs. W. F. Stevens for research; and to my wife, Zellah Endhy Sockman, for counsel and encouragement.

Contents

A short time ago I announced as my theme for a public address, "Man's First Love." I asked a few friends what the subject suggested to them. One said he thought it referred to mother love, because a child's first love is for its mother. A second thought that man's first love is self-love, and he quoted the old adage, "Self-preservation is nature's first law." Two or three others were of the opinion that the theme would be budding romantic love.

Yet, according to the Bible, man's first love is the love of God. The synoptic gospels record the interview of Jesus with the lawyer who asked what is the first commandment in the law. And Jesus' answer was: "You shall love the Lord your God with all your heart, and with all your soul, and with all your mind, and with all your strength."[1]

If that answer seems tame and colorless after what you expected to hear about "Man's First Love," may we hasten to say that, when a person puts the love of God as his first, it makes a vital difference to all his other forms of love. That is why the Scripture puts it first. The love of God is not a pale substitute for romantic love or a pious extra added to love of mate and child and neighbor. It is the fountain of life which refreshes and sustains all our streams of love.

Why at first sound does the command to love God lack interest for the modern reader? For many it seems too vague or too impersonal. For some it appears impossible in view of the injustice which they feel the divine hand has dealt them. For multitudes the difficulty derives from their concept of love. They think of love as a

---

[1] Mark 12:30.

spontaneous affection aroused by the lovableness of an object, and the thought of God just does not stir that kind of feeling. Their minds may experience an occasional glow at the sight of divine handiwork in nature or at the thought of divine justice in history, but their hearts are not warmed by the contemplation of God as First Cause or as Ultimate Value or even as Holy Spirit.

Of course, those who picture God in anthropomorphic form as a bearded grandfatherly being sitting somewhere in the heavens find no problem in loving him as long as all goes well with themselves, but the telescope and the sputnik have destroyed the concept of a six-foot God and confirmed Christ's definition that *"God is spirit."*[2]

After forty years in the Christian ministry the writer is convinced that the vast majority of churchmen are failing to realize the meaning and primacy of the first and great commandment of our faith. And for this reason we are lagging so tragically in fulfilling the second commandment, which Christ set alongside as being equally essential: "You shall love your neighbor as yourself."[3]

This book is written for those who are thoughtful enough to desire deeper reality in their love of God and richer content in their other loves.

---

[2] John 4:24.
[3] Mark 12:31.

PART ONE

1 MAN'S FIRST LOVE

What Is Love?
How Can Love Be Commanded?
Why Is Love the First Command?
To Escape Our Aloneness

What Is Love?

When we talk about man's first love we are forced to ask, first of all, *what is love?* To many this may seem a needless, even a silly question. We assume that we know what love is. It is the feeling aroused in us by some person or object that appeals to us. Hence our concern is simply to find persons to love and conversely to make ourselves attractive and lovable to others.

Yet a little thought reminds us that love is more than this love-seeking and love-making. There is a love which we do not have to seek or make. Mother love is waiting for us ready-made when we come into the world. A normal mother loves her child whether the child be good or bad, homely or beautiful, male or female. Mother love is not to be explained as attraction between sexes or as affinity between similarities.

We sometimes hear it said that we like what is like ourselves and dislike that which is different. Yet it often happens that love seems to be kindled by contrasts. Old persons often dearly love and are loved by children. Learned men frequently have most congenial comradeship with persons of limited knowledge. Nor can we explain love as the desire to possess. Citizens may love their queen or leader, yet the desire is to bless, not to possess.

Love is so deep-seated that it cannot be dug up for definition or complete analysis. Dr. Paul Tillich says: "I have given no definition of love. This is impossible because there is no higher principle by which it could be defined."[1]

Love is a life force, integral to our human nature. Just as the life

---

[1] Unfortunately I am unable to locate the source of this quotation.

force pushes up through the roots of the trees, so love surges through our being, splitting the seeds of the self and pushing out into interpersonal union.

Love is a force within us seeking release rather than a vacuum craving to be filled. We do desire manifestation of affection from our loved ones but true love desires even more to give. And however much he gives, the true lover always feels in debt to the one he loves.

Since the primary motive of love is to give rather than to receive, Erich Fromm, writing from the viewpoint of psychology, asserts that a child never really begins to love until about the age of eight and a half to ten years. Before that age the child responds to love, but at about that time there appears a new feeling of producing love by his own activity. He wants to give something to his father or mother and thus he transforms being loved into loving.

I think that Fromm has put the age of the child too high or else my grandchildren are a bit precocious. (Of course, that is very possible!) But his statement recalls a scene in my daughter's home on a recent Christmas. The presents were piled under the Christmas tree awaiting distribution after breakfast. But while the family was at breakfast the seven-year-old boy slipped shyly up behind his father's chair and put a little letter rack at his plate. It was a gift which he had made at school out of pieces of plywood. The lad was too eager to wait through breakfast until he was to receive his presents. And as I watched the radiant expression of his face I felt I was getting a fresh insight into what Jesus meant when he said, "It is more blessed to give than to receive." And since reading Erich Fromm's book, I wonder if I was not then getting a glimpse of what he would call a man's first love.

That love is a basic life force which seeks outlet in giving is the truth Jesus was trying to tell the woman at the well of Samaria. Her life had been a sordid one. She had had five husbands and the man with whom she was currently living was not her husband. She was drawing the fleeting satisfactions of life from the surface drains, even the gutters. Then Jesus told her of a well of water within, which can spring up into eternal life. He was seeking to open in her life the springs of divine love which could satisfy the thirst of her soul and refresh the streams of her earthly loves.

How Can Love Be Commanded?

Although love is basically giving rather than getting, is not spontaneity the essence of true affection? Is not love kindled rather than commanded? Yes, but kindling differs from spontaneous combustion. Love without control can be a consuming fire. We can love to order. In fact, love must be divinely ordered or it becomes humanly devastating.

One difficulty in discussing the scriptural injunction to love is that in English we use one word to express feelings for which the Hebrew and Greek had several different terms. We trust the reader will here be patient with a bit of exposition.

In the Old Testament there is a Hebrew word to express love as sexual desire. There is also an expression to describe love in friendship, as in the case of David, who laments over his friend Jonathan, crying, "Your love to me was wonderful, passing the love of woman."[1] Then there is a third manifestation of love, as expressed toward non-personal objects: "You love righteousness and hate wickedness."[2]

When we turn to the Greek language we find three words for love.

One is *erao*, which is used to express passionate yearning between persons. The Greeks sang hymns to sensual, demonic Eros, the un-

---

[1] 2 Samuel 1:26.

[2] Psalms 45:7. In general, however, love as used in the Old Testament is an inexplicable personal force. Rooted in the sex life, love finds its proper objects in persons. Where things or occupations are said to be loved, the language seems pale and metaphorical. And it is reasonable to suppose that the ultimate ground and origin of the idea of love are found in the relation of person to person. Everywhere in the Old Testament God's love implies his personality. Hence, Quell holds that the first commandment— "You shall love the Lord your God with all your heart, and with all your soul, and with all your mind, and with all your strength"—might be paraphrased thus: "Thou shalt exert all thy powers, so that love may produce a disposition which will determine thy conduct; the cultivation of thy relationship to the Lord requires the devotion of the whole personality, heart and soul" (Quell in *Bible Key Words* by G. Kittel, New York, 1952).

controllable god. In Eros the Greeks sought ecstasy. Eros raises the
senses above self-control and transports man above himself. Great
tragedians like Sophocles admitted the ecstatic flash which Eros
could create but saw the danger. Some possible implications of love
as *erao* come down to us in our term "erotic." The New Testament
never employs *erao*.

A second Greek word for love is *fileo*. This means the liking or
caring of gods for men, or of friend for friend. It implies warm affection. The New Testament uses the word when it speaks of love
between parent and child, brother and brother, and in intimate circles generally. We reflect the meaning of the term in our adjective
"filial."

And the Greeks had a third word which we translate "love." It
was *agapao*. While *erao* is impulsive, *agapao* is directed by choice
and will. *Erao* seeks in others the satisfaction of its hunger for life;
agapao often means kindness, practical generosity, doing good to
others, all that expresses devoted good will. It is this third word
which the gospel uses when it says, "You shall love the Lord your
God with all your heart," and, "You shall love your neighbor as
yourself." We are not commanded or expected to love God or our
neighbor in the sense of physical passion or even in the sense of
intimate personal affection such as we show to our families. But we
are commanded to devote ourselves in good will to the good of God
and our neighbors.

Bishop Stephen Neill makes a significant distinction in the direction of love. He says that there are two kinds of love. One kind of
love says, "I wish to make my own something that another has and
which it is in his power to give me." The second kind of love says,
"I wish to give something to the other because I love him."[3] In our
normal affections there are some strands of both these types of love.
There are both the desire to get and the desire to give. But the
quality of our love depends on which direction is dominant. In so far
as the prevailing motive in love is to get, it is kindled by the desir-
ableness of the object loved. In so far as the dominating desire is to
give, it is kindled and directed largely by the will and spirit of the

---

[3] Stephen Neill, *The Christian Character* (Association Press, 1955),
p. 21.

one who loves. And since *agapao*, the word used in the command to love God and our neighbor, means a self-giving directed good will, it is a feeling within our power and therefore we can be commanded to exercise it. Hence the first and great commandment means, "You shall direct your heart and soul and mind and strength toward the good of God."

Why Is Love the First Command?

When we hear the word "Christianity," of what do we think? Do we think of Christianity as one of the world's great religions alongside Hinduism and Islam? Do we think of a vast organized movement numbering some six hundred million members, embodied in cathedrals and colleges and monasteries? Or does the word "Christianity" suggest to us a system of creeds and liturgies and moral codes? Well, our thoughts might go off in any or all of these directions, for Christianity embraces a mighty complex of material and spiritual elements.

But in all this vast complexity of Christianity where does one start in defining the primary duties of being a Christian? The founder of Christianity was faced with this question. And it is not surprising, for Jesus grew up in the Hebrew faith and in his day the Jewish law contained some 613 commandments, 365 negative and 248 positive. The devout Jew, confronted by such a welter of laws, felt the need for simplification.

Jewish teachers before Jesus recognized this need. For instance, Hillel gathered all the commandments together in this summary: "Do not unto thy neighbor what is hateful unto thee; that is the whole law. All the rest is commentary."

It was natural, therefore, that the new teacher from Nazareth should be asked what he considered the essential duty among all the religious laws. The occasion of the asking differs in the gospel accounts, but Matthew, Mark, and Luke all record Jesus' answer in substantially the same form.

When a lawyer asked, "Teacher, which is the great commandment in the law?" Jesus answered, "You shall love the Lord your God with all your heart, and with all your soul, and with all your mind.

[Mark adds, "and with all your strength."] This is the great and first commandment. And a second is like it, You shall love your neighbor as yourself." Then Jesus added: "On these two commandments depend all the law and the prophets."[1]

The first commandment which Jesus quoted is from the sixteenth chapter of Deuteronomy and the second is from the nineteenth chapter of Leviticus. Jesus combined the two and called them the core of Christian duty. Why?

One reason is that love is the basic motive of life. In the fourteenth century the story was current of an old woman coming along the streets of Strasbourg, carrying a pail of water and a torch. When asked what she was about, she answered that the water was to put out the fires of hell so that people would not try to be good in order to escape punishment in hell, and the torch was to burn up heaven so that men would be good not for the sake of heavenly reward but for the love of God himself.[2]

Jesus did not talk much about hell. He said enough to reveal his belief in God's justice. He spoke of the outer darkness reserved for those who did not choose the light. But Jesus did not stress the motive of fear. Fear may restrain persons from doing some bad things but it does not lure them toward new and good things. And the late Reverend "Dick" Shepherd of St. Martin's-in-the-Fields, London, was right when he said that being a Christian consists not in refraining from doing things which no gentleman would do anyway, but in doing good things which a mere gentleman might not think to do. Fear is too negative and repressive to be a proper motive for Christian living.

And the old woman in the legend, with her torch to burn up heaven, though of course a caricature, had a point. Jesus did not try to secure followers by stressing earthly or heavenly rewards. To be sure, he did make it clear that God is a Father who keeps faith with His children. He said that our heavenly Father is even more eager than any earthly parent to give good things to His children.

---

[1] Matthew 22:36–40.

[2] Douglas V. Steere, *Prayer and Worship* (Hazen Books, Association Press, 1938), p. 11.

And at the end of his earthly career he said to his disciples, "I go to prepare a place for you . . . that where I am you may be also."[3]

Yet while Jesus gave all this underlying assurance of heaven he did not keep appealing to his hearers to be good for the sake of heavenly reward. He stressed the principle that we are to lose sight of ourselves in helping and saving others. That seems to be the implication of his interview with the rich young man who came asking how he might inherit eternal life. He had kept the commandments from his youth. But Jesus said, "One thing you lack. Go and sell what you have and give to the poor, then come and follow me."[4] As I see it, Jesus was testing the young man's motive. Was he being good for the sake of eternal reward or was he really interested in his fellow men?

The cynic may criticize the Christian's motive as self-interested insurance. When a person becomes a Christian he does take out a life insurance policy. But it should be a policy primarily designed not to insure his own safety and blessings in heaven but to protect and help those he loves here on earth. The primary motive is love— love for God and love for others.

Does this motive seem to run counter to human nature? We commonly accept the saying that self-preservation is nature's first law. But when we see the true self in the light of Christ we see that self-preservation is not achieved by selfishness and self-seeking. The self is made for love and the self can be fulfilled only through love.

Normally we are born into an atmosphere of love and we feel it before we try to define it. A popular magazine some months ago carried the picture of a family at the Thanksgiving dinner table. The young father was carving the turkey. The young mother sat at the other end of the table. Between them were the two sets of grandparents, a little girl of about seven, and a little boy of perhaps five. And then at the mother's elbow in a high chair sat a baby of about a year. The title of the article was the word "Togetherness." Under the picture ran this legend: "She's too little to know about Pilgrim Fathers and Indians. . . . But there's something pretty exciting going on that she does know about. She knows that there's

[3] John 14:2–3.
[4] Matthew 19:21.

a special place for her at that big beautiful table, that the fun and the talk and the belonging-together warmth, . . . even some of the turkey and cranberries . . . are for her too. She knows that what is going on makes her a part of a whole big wonderful family. She may not know the word—but she's beginning to get the idea: Togetherness."

The talk of togetherness is today being carried into shallow and sentimental channels but the feeling of it is the natural healthful air in which life unfolds. Love is the outreach of the self toward completion.

Not only is love the basic motive of life, it is also the basic *method* of life.

We achieve the good life by love rather than by law. To be sure, we need laws to guide us and restrain us at many points. We could hardly trust our traffic to be regulated by pure love. It would be folly to replace our traffic lights and traffic police with signs reading, "Love your neighbor as yourself." When a person gets behind the wheel of a high-powered motorcar the horsepower seems to lessen the heart-power of his brotherly love. We need regulations and enforcement officials but the mere multiplication of them does not make people good.

As soon as laws are passed they call for interpretation. How do they apply? What do they mean? It was these questions of interpretation which led to the multiplication of the old Jewish laws. For example, consider the fourth commandment in the Decalogue: "Remember the sabbath day, to keep it holy . . . in it you shall not do any work." But what is to be considered forbidden work? Is it a violation of the law to travel? To heal the sick? Men even asked, "Is it lawful to tie a knot on the Sabbath?" To such questions the rabbinical regulations gave such answers as these: A Sabbath day's journey is two thousand cubits. A healer may attend a patient on the Sabbath if he is in mortal danger. A person may tie on the Sabbath day any knot which he could untie with one hand. Thus we see how meticulous and detailed lawmaking can become, not only in the ancient Jewish codes but in modern practice among all peoples. It was such casuistry which Jesus tried to correct when he said, "The

Sabbath is made for man and not man for the Sabbath."[5] Useful service is the test of laws. That is one place where love comes in to correct law.

Another weakness of laws is that they cannot cover all concrete situations. Circumstances create exceptions. Dr. G. B. Caird of McGill University says: "Absolute justice demands that a man bear the consequences of his own folly, but few people would be prepared to pursue the logic of this principle so far as to allow a man to starve because he had brought his destitution upon himself. Truthfulness is one of the fundamental moral obligations, but every doctor knows that there are times when it is his duty to tell 'a white lie.' The law requires that we keep a bargain but Shylock has few supporters when he insists on his title to the pound of flesh that was written in his bond."[6]

A further weakness of law is that it can deal only with actual deeds and not with inner motives. In our laws against killing, our penal code distinguishes between killing with premeditation, which is murder, and killing without planned intent, which is homicide, and killing by criminal negligence. But until the killing has taken place the law has nothing to say. How about the case of which Dr. Caird tells? A man so hated his neighbor that he lay in wait for him with a gun on the road by which the neighbor usually returned home. It so happened that the neighbor was sick on this particular day and did not go to work. Hence the man was not guilty in the eyes of the law, but certainly he was guilty in the eyes of Christ. Christ said, "You have heard that it was said to the men of old, 'You shall not kill; and whoever kills shall be liable to judgment.' But I say to you that every one who is angry with his brother shall be liable to judgment."[7]

As Professor John Knox has said, love goes under the laws to reach down to motives, love goes between the laws to cover life situations which the letter of the law does not touch, and love goes beyond

[5] Mark 2:27.

[6] G. B. Caird, *The Truth of the Gospel*, Oxford University Press, 1950, p. 139.

[7] Matthew 5:21-22.

the law to devise new methods and achieve things which laws cannot do.

We can tell the difference when a person is doing something just to keep the law and when he is doing it to keep a love. In 1946, on a mission to Russia, I visited many hospitals and I saw the care given by the state to orphaned children and to those whose mothers were sweeping the streets and laying bricks. With all credit to the efficiency of the government employees in attendance on those little children, it is hard to find a professional worker who can be an adequate substitute for a mother's tender love. Social experts, studying juvenile delinquency, declare that they must have as teachers, judges, policemen, and probation officers persons "who have a feeling for children." It is this "feeling for children," this inner compulsion of love, which goes beyond law—it is this which we need in human relations.

Some time ago a couple appeared in the home term court of New York City. They had been married about ten years and were having trouble. They were trying to explain the situation to the Protestant counselor. Both were seeking to see how little they could yield in order to get by. Contrast their spirit in the courtroom with what must have been their attitude during their courtship, when each was trying to see how much could be done to please the other. When we are merely keeping a law we try to see how little we can do, but when we are keeping a love we try to see how much we can do.

Love goes beyond the law. "Love bears all things, believes all things, hopes all things, endures all things. Love never ends."[8] Because love is life's most basic motive and method, it is the great and first divine command.

To Escape Our Aloneness

"The deepest need of man is the need to overcome his separateness, to leave the prison of his aloneness. The absolute failure to achieve this aim means insanity."[1]

The word "idiot" stems from the Greek term for "private person." How long it would take absolute privacy to produce idiocy is hard

---

[8] 1 Corinthians 13:7–8.

[1] Erich Fromm, *The Art of Living* (New York, 1956), p. 9.

to say, one reason being that absolute aloneness is most difficult to attain. But we all know that keeping too much to ourselves erelong does tend to make us queer.

The person who cuts himself off from all conversation can talk to himself, but talking to oneself gives the impression of queerness and after a while creates a mental quirk. A man can play golf by himself, but my experience on the golf course is that I soon find myself too poor a player to make the game interesting. A person can chuckle to himself but a hearty laugh seldom breaks forth in solitude. A man can sit off alone and laugh *at* others, but wholesome laughter which refreshes the spirit is shared *with* others.

Truly, as the motto of a Greek-letter college fraternity puts it, "One man is no man."

To escape their aloneness, men try all sorts of outlets. Alcohol is one, and bartenders are martyrs to the babble of lonely drinkers. The newsstands are covered with "escape" literature. Many persons become "joiners," thinking that membership in some group will save them from their dread of separateness. Thus campus and community become so cluttered with committees and clubs that residents are left with scanty remnants of time to themselves, and conformity to group patterns of thought limits independence of judgment and lessens individuality of taste.

To be sure, love leads us out of our aloneness into circles of family and friendship. But here, too, inadequacies begin to appear. In T. S. Eliot's *The Cocktail Party,* Celia, the wife, confesses to the psychologist that she finds two symptoms of something wrong with herself. The first is that she feels alone, even though she has a husband, a home, and a crowded schedule of social engagements.

The other symptom is what she calls her feeling of sin. She is not guilty of flagrantly violating the accepted marital code. She and her husband thought that they were giving much to each other but she has come to the conclusion that they "had merely made use of each other, each for his purpose." And that to her now seems horrible.

The wife had learned that true love in marriage cannot be achieved by two persons seeking self-release or self-realization. We should be sufficiently realistic to admit that some element of self-interest enters into marriage. What young groom does not take pride in presenting his bride to his boyhood friends? What bride does not bask in the reflected success of the one she calls "her man"? As has been said above, love has in it two strands: the desire to get and the desire to give. But in true love the latter outweighs the former.

What is more, we human beings in our own wisdom and strength cannot satisfactorily balance this give-and-take of love. We desire to be of use to those we love and yet the relationship is spoiled if we feel that we are being used. We long to give ourselves in loyalty to some person or group, some community or nation, but we are loath to give ourselves away by losing our individuality and independence. We are creatures with the craving to lose ourselves and also to find ourselves.

Another escape from imprisoning aloneness should be mentioned. A person may lose himself in his work with such abandon and zest that for a time he feels complete self-fulfillment. We say that he has found himself in his work. He lives in his work and for his work. There are those who look upon their work as an end in itself. We may not go so far as Emil Brunner and call them "work fanatics." We may applaud them for the creative talent which their absorption releases.

But however interesting and creative our work, it cannot satisfy the soul's hunger for wholeness. However large his bank, a banker cannot put all himself into it. How often it happens that a person who excels in his special line restlessly desires to be a success in some line not his own. And suppose that he does like his work so well that he never looks at the clock. The time comes when he has to look at the calendar. If he has lived only for his job, retirement means retrogression. No man-motivated labor is large enough for the losing and finding of one's whole self.

Jesus Christ made the sweeping claim that he could reconcile this conflict between losing and finding the self. "He who finds his life will lose it, and he who loses his life for my sake will find it."[2] While Jesus at the moment was probably speaking of possible martyrdom, he was stating a principle basic to life on this planet. There is a higher love in which man can lose himself and thereby find himself.

[2] Matthew 10:39.

This is the truth which Christ asserted and which St. Augustine, after much exploration of earthly escapes, discovered and declared: "Thou hast made us for Thyself, O God, and our souls are restless till they find rest in Thee."

Here, then, is the logic of love. Man's first love is to God with all his heart and soul and mind and strength because without this basic love all his human loves leave him unfulfilled.

But man in his aloneness cannot love God. Therefore Christ linked to the first commandment a second "like unto it" in imperative necessity: "You shall love your neighbor as yourself." "On these two commandments hang all the law and the prophets."[3] Yes, and these two commandments must hang together or life falls apart.

---

[3] Matthew 22:40 (King James Version).

The word "heart," as used in Scripture and in common conversation, is hard to define because we make it include so many aspects of experience. "Heart in Hebrew psychology is primarily the seat of the mind and will, together with a whole range of psychical emotions."[1]

Certainly we involve the will when we speak of "putting our heart" into anything. We mean that we set the force of the will to do it. Also the "heart" involves the mind. As Pascal said, "We know the truth, not only by the reason, but also by the heart."

And surely the term "heart" includes the feelings. When we say, "He lost his heart to her," we do not mean exactly that he lost his will or that he lost his mind, although a man in love may sometimes act as if he had lost both! A person may lose his heart in love and yet keep his head in business. But to lose one's heart is to be moved by strong feeling. Hence the commandment, "You shall love the Lord your God with all your heart," involves will and thought, but primarily feeling.

The roots of religion rise out of feeling. This may not necessarily mean visible emotional excitement but it does mean a deep sense of personal concern. It is something that profoundly matters and hence is more than factual knowledge. When Thomas à Kempis declared, "Far rather had I feel a sorrow for my sin than know the definition of it," he was illustrating this distinction. Knowledge about God may be gained by study and instruction, but knowledge of God involves feeling, insight, and intuition.

The "heart" is the seat of the feelings. But it is difficult to define

---

[1] Interpreter's Bible, Vol. 2, p. 374.

what feelings are. They are involved with ideas, yet they are not ideas. They are related to our bodies, yet they are not bodies.

Concern

When we try to analyze the emotions involved, we may say that to love God with your heart begins with a feeling of *concern*. We should start not by asking whether God is but by asking how much we care whether God is.

When a person finishes school, it is more important to ask what subjects he loves than to ask what facts he knows. A student may pass his final examination in a field of study with a fairly high grade, but if he has no love for the subject he is likely to drop it as finished.

Another student who receives a lower grade in the examination may have acquired such an interest in the subject that he goes on to pursue it. Some ninety years ago a boy in Ohio seemed to find learning so difficult that his mother was advised to take him out of school. But the lad had fallen in love with scientific experimentation and he followed his interest until he became the wizard of science known to the world as Thomas A. Edison. The test of an education is not the volume of facts which we master but the value of the loves which master us.

HOW MUCH DO WE CARE? Likewise in religion: how much we care about God is primarily more important than how much we know about God. In his poem, *Bishop Blougram's Apology*, Browning pictures a skeptic troubled by his doubts about some points of the Christian faith. Finally the bishop asks the doubter, "Like you this Christianity or not? . . . Has it your vote to be so if it can?" That is the basic question from which to start in developing our love of God and Christ.

And not only do we care, but how much do we care? In one of Hamlin Garland's poems is this line: "My heart is aflame to be right." He was voicing his burning desire to know the right thing to do in this confused and complicated world. When we note how poets and prophets and saints struggle to find the truth and the right, conventional Christians by contrast seem but light "half-believers of casual creeds." We are content to be good enough to get by with our

crowd and be decently respectable, but our hearts are hardly aflame
to know what is morally or theologically right.

A recent visit to Assisi served to sharpen the contrast between St.
Francis, who hallowed that place, and the contemporary Christian
tourists who visit it. The saint was so concerned over the plight of the
poor that he sacrificed all his earthly prospects to serve them. The
sight-seers first sought the most comfortable hotel accommodations,
then sauntered out to retrace the steps of Francis, to gaze at the
relics of his earthly career, and to admire the frescoes of his ecstatic experiences. The contrast was similar to the difference in
feeling between children and adults on Christmas morning when
Santa Claus dashes into the room to distribute his presents. The
adults go through the motions but not the emotions of the children.

EMOTIONALISM AND EMOTION   Contemporary religion in America
is lacking in genuine emotion. On the one hand are certain shallow
types of religious expression which substitute cheap sentimentalism
for true sentiment. Some lower the noble discourse of prayer into a
chatty talk with "the Man Upstairs," to whom they turn in the midst
of variety shows, even between the rounds of boxing bouts. Some
turn from the stately hymns to "swing" tunes. Some groups still stress
the fear of hell. Others, without much concern for theological
concepts, just "put on the arousements" by any methods which will
evoke an emotional ferment.

On the other hand are those who reduce religion to a sterile intel-
lectualism. They rationalize emotion to the point of destroying it.
They want only the cold facts and try to weigh them with cool
judgment. To such persons religion is a study in logic, not an ad-
venture in love. Between the Scylla of emotional anti-intellectualism
and the Charybdis of unfeeling fact-finding we must steer a course
of Christlike emotion.

Jesus sought to curb outbursts of shallow emotionalism. When a
woman in the crowd raised her voice and cried: "Blessed is the
womb that bore you, and the breasts that you sucked!" he restrained
the outburst by answering, "Blessed rather are those who hear the
word of God and keep it!"[1]

---

[1] Luke 11:27–28.

And Jesus did not seek to arouse emotion by inflammatory picturization of sin and its consequences. He had some hot words for the smug Pharisees, but as a rule he did not play upon his hearers' fears in order to excite their feelings.

Yet Jesus did stir genuine emotion. The purity of his character caused men to feel shame for their sins. The radiance of his goodness made the mediocre virtues of others look like cheap stage jewelry brought into the sunlight. Even Simon Peter was moved by his Master's presence to cry: "Depart from me, for I am a sinful man, O Lord."[2]

And while Jesus aroused in men's hearts an aversion to sin, even more did he move them with an attraction to goodness. He possessed a secret of poised and triumphant living which aroused the curiosity of multitudes and the craving of many. Nicodemus, the learned scribe, came to seek Jesus' formula and apparently never escaped the lure of Our Lord's appeal. A rich young man came "running" to inquire how he might have the kind of life Jesus revealed. Jesus awakened the "better angels" of men's natures. He alerted men's hopes. He made them see stars they never saw before. He set their hearts racing.

With the multitudes Jesus' presence created only a passing emotion. The crowds melted away as they saw that Jesus' preaching did not fit their patriotic patterns. But the more he talked about the cross the more deeply he plowed the hearts of those who continued with him. The scenes at Bethany with his close friends during the last week throb with tender emotion. The centuries have not plumbed the depths of feeling reached in the Last Supper. And while the experience of Christ on the cross was so overwhelming that it seemed to paralyze the emotions of those closest to it, the crucifixion remains the most moving event in human history.

> *See, from His head, His hands, His feet,*
> *Sorrow and love flow mingled down.*
> *Did e'er such love and sorrow meet,*
> *Or thorns compose so rich a crown?*

---

[2] Luke 5:8.

As the light of the sun can be brought to burning focus by the reflection of a mirror, so the love of God is brought to flaming feeling by the compassion and crucifixion of Jesus Christ. When we behold God's grace in nature, we may feel a "Presence which disturbs us with the joy of elevated thoughts"; when we contemplate God's providence in personal and national situations, we may feel a profound gratitude. But when we see Christ on the cross praying for those whose nails were piercing his own palms, we stand with the saints seeking to "comprehend . . . the breadth and length and height and depth and to know the love of Christ which surpasses knowledge."[3]

Only as concepts are brought to personal focus do they come home to the hearts of the people. We have certain high moods, which can be stirred by contemplating the universal love of God or the abstract blessing of liberty or the general suffering of mankind. But by and large such concepts become vital to us only when they emerge from the vagueness of the general into the particular and the personal. We read with only casual concern of whole battalions bombed in Korea, of thousands rotting as refugees in Jordan, of hundreds killed in highway traffic. And then a little boy falls into a dry well and the papers of the whole nation portray every detail of his plight while people watch with bated breath and fervent prayer the efforts to rescue him.

Some years ago Aldous Huxley said that modern means of communication had made us so repeatedly aware of the world's sufferings that we have grown callous to them. So it would seem. Then comes a poignant personal experience which gets under our callous skins. Bernard Shaw, in *Saint Joan*, represents a priest, who had witnessed the execution of Joan of Arc, saying to his bishop that a person must see such things in order to be changed by them. The bishop replies: "Must then a Christ be crucified in each generation to save those who have no imagination?"

Commitment
Visits to college campuses reveal an increasing interest in religion. Students criticize many contemporary manifestations of religion as

---

[3] Ephesians 3:18–19.

superficial and sentimental, but alert young minds are waking up to the fact that they cannot consider themselves educated unless they know something about religion, the force which has inspired the richest art, produced the noblest characters, and gripped the world's masses. Students may not be concerned enough to get up for college chapel but most of them are interested enough to remain up till midnight to discuss religion in "bull sessions." And more college courses are being given in the religious field than ever before.

Yet, while they are interested in studying about religion, students are skeptical about committing themselves to any one body of believers. Is there not some good in all the great religions? Why not keep the mind open to the values in the various faiths? Why is it not enough to study religions comparatively and take the best of each without narrowing our minds in devotion to any one?

Such reasoning seems plausible and broad-minded. And truly we should keep our minds open to every vista of truth, and we should remember that truth is too vast for any one religious body to claim a monopoly. Christian sects should be humbled into tolerance of one another by Christ's own words: "I have other sheep, that are not of this fold."[1] And Christianity should recognize that God has not limited his revelation to Judaeo-Christian channels.

Nevertheless, just as the beauty of a stained-glass window in a church can be seen only by those who view it from inside the building, so the merits of a religion can be fully appraised only by those who commit themselves to its counsels and demands. That is why converts from one religious body to another are seldom made by interfaith conferences.

One reason why we have to commit ourselves to a religion before we can know it is that we learn to know persons in a different way from that in which we learn to know things. If we want to know the truth about a non-personal object or subject, we assemble the facts and then make up our minds. But in dealing with persons we reach a point where we must make a decision and then let the future reveal more facts. In love, in friendship, even in forming a business partnership or hiring an employee, we come to the place where we

---

[1] John 10:16.

must make a choice on faith. In dealing with impersonal facts, we can be sure before we commit ourselves. In dealing with persons, we must commit ourselves before we can be sure.

In our Christian faith there is a knowledge of things to be gained by a study of facts just as in a schoolroom. But remember also that in getting to know God as Our Heavenly Father and Jesus Christ as Our Lord and Savior we are dealing with persons and hence we have to commit ourselves.

THE LIMITATIONS OF THE OPEN MIND   We see this principle of commitment in realms other than religion. For example, in music we often hear people say, "I am not musical but I am fond of music," or "I do not play or sing but I love music." But can we really love music unless we try to sing or play?

Sir Hugh Allen, conductor of the Oxford Bach choir, expressed a teacher's insight when he said, "Whatever is worth doing, is worth doing badly." We learn by doing even if we do it badly. If we are studying voice, we do not merely go around hearing great singers. We have to put ourselves in the hands of some teacher and submit to his regimen. Jesus, therefore, was following the practice of any true teacher when he said, "Take my yoke upon you, and learn from me."[2] His dictum may sound narrow and dogmatic. What free mind wants to be yoked? But the paradox of freedom is that we achieve the full free use of our minds and bodies by committing ourselves through discipline and devotion to something or someone great enough to develop our self-fulfillment.

The little girl at the piano at first feels the finger exercises a drudgery. They seem a restriction on her liberty. She has a hard time "getting the hang" of those musical scores. But after a while the music begins to get her. Cheap tunes can be caught from a juke box but the appreciation of great music requires commitment, cultivation, and much living with.

There are realms in which the eclectic attitude of keeping uncommitted and selecting what seems best does not work. In religion, as in marriage or in music, we must commit ourselves and make a start if we are to learn to love God and feel his power.

---

[2] Matthew 11:29.

This urge to commitment may come after long reflection and testing experience or it may come in adolescence. A young girl of fifteen from a sophisticated New York family attended one of the Billy Graham evangelistic meetings in Madison Square Garden. When the evangelist gave the appeal to come forward at the close of the meeting, she was moved to go. The reason she gave is revealing. She said that she had gone through the church school of a prominent Protestant Episcopal parish and that it was "in the cards for her to be confirmed in the next class." But she said, "I have never felt anything. Tonight I feel I want to give my heart to Christ." Some may explain her "feeling" as the contagion of the crowd emotion. Men may criticize the high-pressure methods of presenting the gospel and the self-centered motives of appeal, but the fact remains that something ignited the vital spark of commitment in that adolescent girl's spirit. Unless somewhere along the line our church programs kindle that spark, they fail.

THE WEAKNESS OF THE INDECISIVE CHURCH   So essential is the commitment of the will in learning to love God that Kant centers religious need and trust in the will, as Hegel centers it in reason, and Schleiermacher in feeling. Each is partly right and partly wrong. Yet in stressing the will Kant is in line with Jesus' own teaching. When his Jewish critics asked, "How is it that this man has learning, when he has never studied?" Jesus answered, "My teaching is not mine, but his who sent me; if any man's will is to do his [God's] will, he shall know whether the teaching is from God or whether I am speaking on my own authority."[3] Conduct shapes belief quite as much as belief shapes conduct. Read the New Testament and note the frequent use of the word "walk." "Walk in the light," "walk in newness of life." There is new truth to be explained in the old expression, "falling head over heels in love," because in the love both of persons and of God we often progress feet first rather than head first.

Not only are commitment and action necessary steps in loving God, but their absence is actually demoralizing. To be emotionally stirred or to be confronted by a challenge and then to do nothing about it is disintegrating to character. That is the truth with which

---

[3] John 7:15-17.

Matthew's gospel concludes the collected sayings of Jesus, called the Sermon on the Mount. ". . . every one who hears these words of mine and does not do them will be like a foolish man who built his house upon the sand; and the rain fell, and the floods came, and the winds blew and beat against that house, and it fell."[4]

Herein lies a basic weakness in conventional religion. In our weekly sermons we echo Our Lord's commands and confront congregations with moral challenges. But we do not integrate these into our lives by obedience and action. In our sacraments and liturgies we retrace the scenes of Our Lord's suffering and sacrifice to people ever seeking to be more comfortable. On Good Friday we gather in great numbers to hear the words from the cross and so often we measure the success of the service by the size of the attendance and the eloquence of the participants.

Our church services are lacking in dramatic power, as critics are ever deploring. Nevertheless, they are patterned after the theater. The minister and the choir are on the stage, the congregation are the spectators. When the service is over, any emotion which may have been stirred is allowed to evaporate in conversation. No convictions are clinched by commitment of will. No quickened interests are resolved into action. Another "service" is over.

Because our regular church services lack this element of commitment they leave the way open for the traveling revivalist. The evangelist may not make much contribution to the content of religion. His theology may be antiquated but his old-fashioned appeals for decision strike a responsive chord in the hearts of churchmen who have been missing it. He calls for commitment on the part of churchmen who have been mere spectators.

We do well to ponder Kierkegaard's conception that primarily in a service of worship the preacher is not the actor and the people the audience, but the worshipers are the actors and God is the audience. We, the people, are in church to do things before God. The preacher is the prompter off stage who directs our thoughts and words. We present our hearts and minds, our souls and bodies to be "a living

---

[4] Matthew 7:26–27.

sacrifice, holy and acceptable to God, which is your spiritual worship."[5]

A service of worship is primarily a service to God. When we realize this and act upon it, we make it a service to men.

Conversion

To commit the will to God does not guarantee loving God with all the heart. The heart is so inclusive that it contains many compartments. One room of the heart may be warmed with love of God while others may remain cold. Religious conversion is a progressively pervasive process.

This is a fact which America's evangelism overlooked for a long time. In my boyhood I was familiar with revival services which were quite regularly conducted in rural and small-town parishes each winter. Usually quite a number "gave their hearts to Christ" each season. But during the summer many of these lapsed in their spiritual enthusiasm. These were called "backsliders." (This is a term not commonly heard in our modern parishes; the reason may be that our contemporary parishioners do not get far enough ahead to slide back!)

Modern evangelists are trying to check this ecclesiastical loss by a businesslike system of follow-up. The "inquirer" or "convert" is assigned to some church, enrolled in some organization, perhaps given some scripture passages which he pledges himself to read. But however briskly efficient such methods of professionalized cultivation, they are not sufficient to develop commitment of will into conversion of life.

THE TASTE AS WELL AS THE WILL   For one thing, a person may be committed in will and yet not converted in taste. Like Prince Hal, he may vow to be kingly but his tastes are still down on the level of Falstaff. A person is not fitted for the Christian life until he has learned to like what Jesus liked. A virtue is never safe until it is transformed from duty into desire.

And certainly the conversion of taste is essential for eternal living. Christ's promise is: "I go to prepare a place for you. And when I go

---

[5] Romans 12:1.

and prepare a place for you, I will come again and will take you to myself, that where I am you may be also."[1] To be where Christ is and not to like what Christ likes will not be heaven, but quite the opposite. The difference between heaven and hell is a matter of taste rather than of temperature.

It is not true that we "needs must love the highest when we see it." Our best tastes require cultivation. We do not always like at first sight the things that later prove most worth while. Many a happily married couple did not fall in love at first sight. A person cannot saunter in from the sidewalk level of sensational scenarios and night clubs and expect immediate enjoyment of a truly religious service. It takes time to adjust the eyes of the mind to the religious light of divine perception. St. Paul prayed for the Ephesians: that, "having the eyes of your hearts enlightened, . . . you may know what is the hope to which he [God] has called you."[2] This heart vision is a deep insight which requires contemplation and cultivation.

Critics of the church often miss this point. Admitting the dullness of many conventional religious services, we still declare that multitudes are not giving the churches a fair chance to test the appeal of religion. They sample the church services so casually and infrequently that they do not get into the atmosphere of godliness. They do not hold themselves long enough in that stillness which feels the heartbeat of the Eternal. They do not give time for their minds to take hold of "whatever is true, whatever is honorable . . . just . . . pure . . . lovely . . . gracious."[3]

When the psalmist cried, "O taste and see that the Lord is good!"[4] he was speaking out of long and rich experience.

THROUGH DUTY TO DESIRE   The goodness of God is not always apparent at the first taste. Worship is only one aspect of our contact with God but it will suffice to illustrate. The first contacts with religious groups are not always exciting or even interesting. The first participation in a church service is not always pleasant. In fact the

---

[1] John 14:2-3.
[2] Ephesians 1:18.
[3] Philippians 4:8.
[4] Psalms 34:8.

taste for religious services has to be acquired somewhat as does the taste for good music. And in the process of acquirement there may be periods of dullness and drudgery. Just as the student of music has to go through the uninspiring drills, so there are times of forced effort in cultivating a taste for religious exercises. The love of God usually has to pass through the stage of duty before it becomes desire.

Henry C. Link, the psychologist, in his book, *The Return to Religion*, frankly confessed his dislike of going to church. He wrote: "I go to church because I would rather lie in bed late on Sunday mornings, the only chance for a good sleep I have during the week. I go because I would rather read the Sunday papers. I go because I know it will please my old father, when he learns of it, and my parents-in-law, whom I shall undoubtedly see there. I go because I shall have to meet and have to shake hands with people, many of whom do not interest me in the least; because if I don't go, my children consider that they have a good reason for not going to Sunday school; because I might be asked to do something I don't want to do: because I may disagree with what the minister has to say. . . . I go because I do not believe in all the doctrines of this church, or any other church. I go, in short, because I hate to go and because I know that it will do me good."[5]

The psychologist was no doubt overcoloring a bit to prove his point. But his point is sound. Part of the value of religion is found in the discipline of doing things which at first are unpleasant. If we do only what we like to do, we are in danger of deteriorating to the disillusionment expressed by a young American émigré of the Paris Left Bank who confessed: "We took what we liked until we no longer liked what we took." Unless we resist the gravity of our lower tastes with a forced lift to the acquirement of higher tastes, life becomes "stale, flat and unprofitable."

BRINGING PERSONAL VIRTUES UP TO DATE   Social attitudes as well as tastes need to be brought into the orbit of conversion. A man may give his heart to God in personal commitment of will and yet not comprehend at all what this implies in his business and social re-

---

[5] H. C. Link, *The Return to Religion* (New York, 1936), p. 19.

lationships. That is why it is naïve to say that if we can just convert individuals to Christ we shall have a Christian world. A person may "come to Christ" with his physical passions brought under moral control and yet his political views may be completely untouched by Christian considerations. He may keep the Ten Commandments and yet have no concern about the tens of millions who are suffering today from the breaking of these laws. A man may be correct in his creeds and unconverted in his pocketbook.

Some years ago a well-known industrialist pyramided his financial speculations until they collapsed, dragging down uncounted fortunes and causing several suicides. In an address which I made at that time I referred a bit critically to the man and his business operations. At the close of my message a woman came up to me and said, "I am sorry that you criticized Mr. ———. He summers near me on the Massachusetts coast. I am sure that he would not harm anybody he knew." Maybe the lady was right in saying that the refined gentleman would not steal from anyone he knew. But in our long-range complex world we can steal from many we do not know and we can do it in such diluted forms that even our own consciences do not hurt us. If we are going to teach honesty today, we must teach it not only for the simple hand-to-hand dealings of the village store but also for the invisible far-ranging transactions of the stock market and international exchange.

To love God with the whole heart means bringing the old personal virtues up to the frontiers of our new social temptations. A point worth noting is that, while church statistics are at an all-time high, the United States is also breaking its crime records. Over two and a half million major crimes were committed in this country during 1956.

Moreover, some of the most rapid advances in church membership are being made in sections where racial segregation is proving most troublesome. Multitudes are not yet translating their love of God into wholesome racial attitudes. Contemporary revivalism is far from begetting a consecration of the whole heart.

Timely and imperatively important is the recent report of the committee on evangelism to the National Council of Churches. Its delineation outlines the wholeness of religious conversion. "Evangelism is making the gospel known to those who do not know it, in hope that they may be turned to God in faith, and making it more effectively known to those who already live within the church, that their faith may grow in clarity and strength. Evangelism, thus understood, is very different from the revivalism that seeks, by exhortation and perhaps by emotional pressure, to induce voluntary decision almost as an end in itself. . . . Evangelism is a continuing task in many varied forms: prophetic and homiletic witness; theological clarification, inquiry and defense; formal and informal nurture, biblical and catechetical teaching; corporate and individual counselling—all to the end that God in Christ may be more fully and powerfully known."[6]

When we thus look at the process of conversion as a task of the church, we see what a manifold operation it is. It requires varied programs, co-ordinated departments, trained personnel. But for the individual concerned personal commitment to Christ cannot deteriorate into the dry dissection of a committee report. Conversion is an experience of the warmed heart, the glowing face, the radiant spirit. Conversion is not a mere change of "this and that," it is an "I-Thou" relationship.

Jesus Christ is more than a mere model that we are to copy as a painter copies a pattern. The attempt to copy Christ is beyond our human strength and soon leads to despair. We are to be rooted and grounded in his love and grow in his grace. J. B. Phillips, whose "Letters to Young Churches" shows his understanding of the Christian faith when it was young and vital, writes: "Unhappily in our day the Christian religion is all too often reduced to a performance to please an external God, while to the early Christians it was plainly the invasion of their lives by a new quality of life—nothing less than the life of God Himself."[7]

The qualities of life which we need and seek to make us whole in heart and life are "love, joy, peace, patience, kindness, goodness, faithfulness, gentleness, self-control." These are the fruit of the

---

[6] Obtained at National Council of Churches, 297 Fourth Avenue, New York, N.Y.

[7] J. B. Phillips, *Making Men Whole* (London, 1955), p. 89.

Spirit.[8] They grow in the life which is open to the invasion of God's love.

It does take decisive effort of will to commit our lives to God in Christ. It may often require tiring and uninspired periods of discipline to train our tastes. But when our self-centered hearts are opened to let God's love in, the fruit of the divine Spirit begins to appear. Religious experience is transformed from a gritting of the teeth to a growing in grace.

FROM LAW TO GRACE   The Bible closes with the words: "The grace of the Lord Jesus be with all the saints."[9] And it has been. Only the grace of God as revealed in Christ has kept the Bible the living word in a living church.

What do we mean by "the grace of the Lord Jesus"? In seeking the deeper theological answers, let us not overlook his grace of manner. We do not know how Jesus looked. He may or may not have been tall and graceful in body. Yet he must have been attractive in the way he bore himself because he drew not only the sick but strangers and little children. He had a grace of speech which could often disarm the fears of those who were honestly suspicious of him.

Such grace of manner is not a mere gloss on the surface of Christian conduct. It is the outward manifestation of a genuine graciousness of spirit. Winsomeness of manner is an important factor in awakening men to love God. Graceless religious attitudes have closed many approaches to godliness. In one of Strindberg's plays a nurse, who is a very ardent churchgoer, is trying to convert an old sea captain, who is an agnostic. As she is talking to him on one occasion he says something like this: "It is strange that when you begin to talk about God and his love, your voice grows hard and your eyes fill with hate." Jesus flamed forth in righteous indignation against evil, but his eyes never filled with hate against persons.

And he had the grace to enter into sympathy with sinful people. One day as he was entering Jericho he saw a dishonest publican named Zacchaeus. Jesus went to dine with this despised countryman. As he was leaving, after Zacchaeus had confessed and pledged

---

[8] Galatians 5:22.
[9] Revelations 22:21.

repayment of his false exactions, Jesus said, "Today salvation has come to this house, since he also is a son of Abraham."[1] To be called a "son of Abraham" was tonic to the publican's soul. It meant that Jesus still regarded him as a Jew worthy of honor and not as a scorned outcast. It has been said that the Beatitudes in the Sermon on the Mount should have another added, namely, "Blessed are they who give us back our self-respect." Jesus restored self-respect to the sinners he converted.

Jesus' graciousness of spirit included tact which could untangle embarrassing situations. On one occasion Jesus and his disciples were at dinner when a woman of questionable reputation made her way in and began to anoint the Master's feet with precious ointment. The disciples at once remonstrated, saying: "Why this waste? For this ointment might have been sold for a large sum, and given to the poor." That seemed a very reasonable question in the light of Jesus' oft-expressed injunction to help the suffering poor. But Jesus saw the woman's embarrassment and he understood the depth and sincerity of the gratitude which she was expressing by her lavish anointing. And he said to his disciples, "Why do you trouble the woman? For she has done a beautiful thing to me."[2]

These situations are cited to remind us that the grace of Jesus Christ made him considerate of all kinds and conditions of men, made him able to put his ear down to those less mentally tall without showing his stoop, made him able to slow his pace for those of feebler strength without seeming to be holding back, made him able to help without hurting and to be hurt without hating.

Such grace is needed if people are to be saved. This is the truth which the prophet Isaiah saw when he was foretelling the coming Deliverer. Isaiah said of the Coming One: "A bruised reed he will not break, and a dimly burning wick he will not quench."[3] How admirably Jesus fulfilled that pattern. The fourth gospel records the scene of the woman taken in the sin which called for stoning. Jesus did not join with the crowd in harsh condemnation, which would have crushed her like a bruised reed. At first he looked at the ground

---

[1] Luke 19:9.
[2] Matthew 26:8–10.
[3] Isaiah 42:3.

and made some marks in the sand. Thus he avoided adding to the woman's distress by looking at her. After this pause he raised his eyes, looked at the crowd, and said, "Let him who is without sin . . . be the first to throw a stone." No one threw. Then Jesus did look at her and said, "Has no one condemned you? . . . Neither do I condemn you; go, and do not sin again."[4] Thus Jesus kept the flickering light of hope from going out in that woman's life. With his sympathetic understanding he cupped the smoking wick of her faith until it flared again into brightness.

The grace of Jesus is highlighted when seen in contrast with the methods and message of John the Baptist, whose integrity and courage merited the Master's tribute that "among those born of women none is greater than John."[5] Yet the flaming forerunner failed to catch the secret of divine grace as available to him "who is least in the kingdom of God." John was remote and ascetic; Jesus mingled with people and made friends. John hurled his warnings down on the heads of his listeners; Jesus took little children up in his arms. John pictured a judgment that made people want to hide for safety; Jesus moved his hearers out of their darkened existence into the sunshine of hope. John was tense, hurrying impatiently toward his goal; Jesus took time to talk with the weary by the wayside and to join with families at wedding feasts. And Jesus said to his followers, "He who has seen me has seen the Father. . . . I am in the Father and the Father in me."[6] Hence the grace we see in Jesus is a reflection of the grace to be seen in God.

Consider the grace of God, that unmerited favor which God grants to his children, over and above what law and justice require. We glimpse this extra goodness of God in nature. By nature's physical laws we can predict the hour of the sunset, even to the minute; but who can foretell its colors? This evening the western horizon may be adorned in gorgeous red; tomorrow night its garment may be a purple robe flecked with gold. These glorious colors are not absolutely necessary to sustain man's bodily health. The alternation of light and darkness would suffice for that. But the Creator throws in sunset

---

[4] John 8:7–11.
[5] Luke 7:28.
[6] John 14:9, 11.

patterns as extras, wrapping up our days in gay colors somewhat as we tie gift packages at Christmas.

Or we think of what theologians term "prevenient grace." The psalmist addresses God, saying, "Thou dost meet him with goodly blessings."[7] Only a little reflection is required to remind us of the spirit of goodness which prepares the way in advance of our coming —the homes which welcome our birth with eager hopes and tender hands, the ancestors who have lived not entirely for themselves and have left something over to enrich the earth, the laws and liberties which we inherit. However heavy our taxes and social responsibilities, we are all wards of divine charity.

Consider also the grace which predisposes us to good things in advance. One of our most beautiful prayers of invocation begins, "Almighty God, from whom every good prayer cometh." Where do our prayers start? Who puts it into our hearts to desire the good things for which we should pray? Whence come the hunger and thirst after righteousness? St. Augustine voiced the secret when he said, "I would not seek Thee hadst Thou not already found me."

History also reveals God's grace. God created a law-abiding universe. He placed man on the earth and endowed him with talents superior to all other animals in order that he might have dominion over the earth. He sent lawmakers to prescribe the rules of living and prophets to interpret them. Certainly that would seem all that justice required. But God did more. "God so loved the world that he gave his only Son, that whoever believes in him should not perish but have eternal life."[8]

But when it is asserted that both nature and history manifest the grace of God, immediate protests are voiced. Can God be called gracious when he sends tornadoes and earthquakes, drought which dries up the soil and dust storms which blow it away; snakes and poisons, viruses and polio victims? Talk about the good God sending more than the law requires? That would seem to be tragically less.

More will be said on this matter when we come to consider the mystery of evil. But no easy explanation should be attempted. Like

---

[7] Psalms 21:3.
[8] John 3:16.

Job, we cannot fathom all the mysteries of the vast, complex universe, but we see so much of the order and grandeur of creation that we are impelled to trust it beyond our sight. In my boyhood I was taught that the colors of the spectrum run from red at one end to violet at the other. Later I learned how much more range of color there is from the infra-red to the ultra-violet. Likewise the experience of faithful living leads us to discover, with Frederick Faber, that:

> *There's a wideness in God's mercy*
> *Like the wideness of the sea;*
> *There's a kindness in his justice*
> *Which is more than liberty.*

And then we think of those who have descended most deeply into the darkness of suffering without losing the light of faith.

Here is a point to be noted. The writer of the Bible's last book, who talks about "the grace of our Lord Jesus Christ," was himself a refugee. A significant fact which fortifies my faith in God is that those who would seem to have the most reason to doubt his goodness are the ones who believe it most firmly.

We are not made responsive to God's grace by hearing someone else talk about it. We have to learn by experience. The New Testament injunction is: "Grow in the grace and knowledge of our Lord and Savior Jesus Christ."[9]

WHEN LOVE BECOMES WHOLEHEARTED   We have all watched little children grow in grace. At first the infant is awkward in taking his first steps. He tumbles and falls. One might read to him a whole treatise on Greek dancing. It would not help him one iota in walking. What the child needs in order to get through his awkward stage is a nursery floor on which to walk and a mother or nurse to help him.

Likewise in learning to understand the grace of God and Our Lord Jesus Christ we must grow into it through personal practice in the situations immediately around us. Thomas Carlyle was right when he said that, if we do the duty next to us and then the duty next after that, it is amazing how the light begins on the ultimate duty.

---

[9] 2 Peter 3:18.

In line with this principle Jesus said to his would-be followers, "Take my yoke upon you, and learn from me; for I am gentle and lowly in heart."[1] Christ's yoke does not seem easy at first. A young friend of mine, who has lost her husband and now her good position, is not finding it easy to believe in God's grace or to carry on in his work. But on the basis of tested experience through the ages I confidently predict that if she does carry on valiantly she will come through victoriously to a firmer and richer faith than she had before.

The Apostle Paul suffered an affliction which he called his "thorn in the flesh." He prayed to have it removed. It remained, but Paul's prayer was answered by the divine assurance, "My grace is sufficient for you, for my power is made perfect in weakness."[2] And it was, for Paul discovered that "suffering produces endurance, and endurance produces character, and character produces hope, and hope does not disappoint us, because God's love has been poured into our hearts through the Holy Spirit which has been given us."[3]

And through his trying experience he came to the conclusion that "love bears all things, believes all things, hopes all things, endures all things. Love never ends."[4] "Who shall separate us from the love of Christ? Shall tribulation, or distress, or persecution, or famine, or nakedness, or peril, or sword? . . . No, in all these things we are more than conquerors through him who loved us."[5]

And when Paul nears the end of his course and is passing the torch to his young understudy, Timothy, he declares triumphantly, "I know whom I have believed and I am sure that he is able to guard until that Day what has been entrusted to me."[6] There speaks one who had grown in the grace and knowledge of the Lord and Savior Jesus Christ, coming valiantly through the hardest struggles of this world into a victorious assurance of God's continued goodness in the world to come. In response to such divine love Paul had come to love the Lord with all his heart.

---

[1] Matthew 11:29.
[2] 2 Corinthians 12:9.
[3] Romans 5:3–5.
[4] 1 Corinthians 13:7–8.
[5] Romans 8:35, 37.
[6] 2 Timothy 1:12.

The Organizer of the Ego

Sometimes we say of a person, "He does not know his own mind." We mean that he is undecided or even that he is unstable. But when we stop to think about it, who does know his own mind? Does any reader feel competent to explain how his mind works, how sights and sounds impinge on his nerves and start trains of thought? No one of us knows how much strength his mind can summon in an emergency.

Nor do any of us know how bad we can be. After a crime of passion a wrongdoer looks at the wreckage wrought by his deed and cries: "How could I have done that?" Strange demonic powers seem to take possession of our minds and mysterious possibilities of sinfulness are revealed within us.

We are told that our minds resemble icebergs in that the main part is submerged below the line of visibility. In this hidden part of the mind, which we call the unconscious, the most potent forces of our nature reside. Barbara Morgan asserts: "To put the intellect at the helm of the mind, of its fancies, its humor, its aspirations, is like using a knife to play the violin. Certainly the instrument of direction is not the emotions either; that way lies chaos. If the mind is ever to harmonize its own efforts, to have power over itself, it will not be through any part of its ruling the whole, but by a distillation of all its fecund energies in what we call spirit."[1]

The first and great commandment reads: "You shall love the Lord your God with all your heart, and with all your soul, and with all

---

[1] Barbara Morgan, *Man's Restless Search* (New York, 1947), p. 60.

your mind, and with all your strength." Some may deem it unwarranted to read into Hebrew psychology any clear-cut distinction between the words "heart," "mind," and "soul." The point of the command is to stress that we are to love God with our whole natures. Perhaps, then, we should not attempt to separate the soul sharply from the heart and mind. Nevertheless, in common usage the words do carry different connotations. To lose one's heart, to lose one's soul, to lose one's mind do not mean the same thing. A person may lose his mind by derangement but we would not say that thereby he has lost his soul.

What is the soul? Biologists assume an inner directive power which they call the "organizer" to account for the way the cells of the body function. May the psychologists not parallel the biologists in assigning the control of the mind to an "organizer" called the spirit?

Baron von Hügel, the mystic, said the soul is a force or energy. Others, baffled by the attempt to define the soul psychologically or physically, say that it is "a bit of divinity": "Man possesses a double nature, a phenomenal ego and an eternal Self, which is the inner man, the spirit, the spark of divinity within the soul."[2] And they are in line with St. Paul writing to the Corinthians: "Do you not know that you are God's temple and that God's Spirit dwells in you?"[3]

But while we cannot locate the residence of the soul, Evelyn Underhill, who was such a perceptive interpreter of things spiritual, wrote a little book some years ago entitled, *The House of the Soul*. She said that the soul lives in a two-story house. As souls, we have a ground floor, a natural life biologically conditioned with animal instincts and affinities. This ground floor is important and not to be left untended. But we have also an upper floor, a supernatural life, with a capacity for God.

If we try to live on only one floor we destroy the mysterious beauty of life. The Prodigal Son lived for a time on the lower floor of his nature, feeding on the husks of the swineherd. But he could not stay content on that level. He "came to himself" and arose and went to his father.

---

[2] Aldous Huxley, *Introduction to Bhagavad-Gita* (New York, 1951), p. 13.
[3] 1 Corinthians 3:16.

On the other hand ascetics try to live entirely on the upper floor of their natures, cut off from contacts with the physical world. The pillar saints in fifth-century Syria symbolized their aloofness from earth's soiling associations by taking up their abode atop stone pillars. Asceticism has had its devotees in every age and in all the great faiths. Jesus did not endorse separation from the practical concerns of society. He said to his disciples, "You are the salt of the earth." Salt mingles with its surroundings in order to savor and save that with which it is mixed. Yet it must not lose its savor, for "how shall its saltness be restored?"[4]

At the end of his earthly ministry Jesus reiterated this point in his prayer for his followers: "I do not pray that thou shouldst take them out of the world, but that thou shouldst keep them from the evil one."[5] The Christian is to be in the world and yet not of the world. "Do not be conformed to this world but be transformed by the renewal of your mind, that you may prove what is the will of God, what is good and acceptable and perfect."[6]

The full wholesome life must have its ground floor with its practical duties and social responsibilities and also its upstairs with its spiritual perspectives which give renewing power.

From Oversoul to Soul

There are times when earth-bound mortals get what they call an inspiration. The narrow matter-of-fact workaday experience is suddenly flooded and transformed by the inrush of a vast experience as from another world. Something seems to break in on the familiar tenor of the person's thoughts. There seems to be an unexpected appearance in the mind of something strikingly different from its habitual course and general contents.

Nothing is more certain than that some persons at some moments are carried beyond the usual range of their thoughts and arrive at insights which seem to be given them from a higher wisdom. Sometimes these flashes of insight come like sudden meteors which leave behind only a brief train of fading light; and sometimes they come

---

[4] Matthew 5:13.
[5] John 17:15.
[6] Romans 12:2.

to persons able by their literary power to preserve them. "Those who have become true children of God and are reborn of the Spirit . . . receive from the spirit of God many and various favors and activities. Sometimes, like guests at a royal feast, they are satiated with indescribable enjoyments; sometimes they are filled with a divine and intimate delight, like that of a bride when she rejoices in the presence of a bridegroom. . . . Sometimes they are seized by a lively compassion at the sight of human misery, and in the ardor of their charity, they give themselves wholly to prayer and tears begging the Divine Mercy for the whole human race. . . . At other times he immerses himself in a profound silence; and then his soul enjoys great peace, and tastes in its quietude of ineffable delights."[1]

These mystical experiences of the divine presence and love may seem so far beyond the range of ordinary daily living that we do not take them into account. In fact our current down-to-earth presentation of religion tends to discount them. One of the most serious weaknesses of the modern church is the failure to cultivate the mystical.

Yet the reality of these moments when "deep calleth unto deep" is being attested on every side. A woman of my acquaintance some time ago went through deep sorrow. She immersed herself in the writings of Evelyn Underhill, Baron von Hügel, and mystics of earlier date. She learned the secret of entering into the stillness; she practiced the art of "recollection," she looked on the things that are unseen and eternal until they became to her realities requiring no proof.

When we look more deeply into these flashes of mystical insight we find that they are not wholly intrusions from without; they seem to be sparks igniting something within the person. Man's rational mind becomes a sort of conductor between the Oversoul and the Unconscious. He is carried away in the spirit. He is in the hands of One "able to do far more abundantly than all that we ask or think."[2] While it is not intended that we should count on this direct aid of the

---

[1] Macarius, Homily XVIII, 7–9.
[2] Ephesians 3:20.

divine Spirit as a substitute for our own straight hard thinking, yet it does supplement our efforts. "When they deliver you up, do not be anxious how you are to speak or what you are to say; for what you are will be given to you in that hour; for it is not you who speak, but the Spirit of your Father speaking through you."[3]

We are less inclined to discount these divine flashes of religious insight when we consider their resemblance to the insights of the poet, the artist, even the scientist. "Poetry," said Shelley, "redeems from decay the visitations of divinity in man."[4]

Dr. Ross A. Baker, a distinguished chemist, some years ago made a study of what is called the "scientific hunch." After consulting more than two hundred scientists he learned that over half of them had experienced these flashes of inspiration which reveal that our minds are not little self-starting, self-sustaining machines grinding observable data into ideas. When the mind is tuned to the search for truth, and keeps tuned, asking, seeking, knocking, it finds something greater than itself moving upon it.

Up from the armies of laboratory technicians rise from time to time men with sufficient insight and imagination to transform data into discoveries. They are the seers of science. When asked how he had discovered the law of gravity, Sir Isaac Newton replied: "By thinking about it continuously. I keep the object of my research constantly before me, waiting until the first light begins to dawn, little by little; finally this changes and at last the light is complete."[5] In our respect for science let us not overlook its debt to imagination and intuition.

From Problem to Mystery

The mystic's contemplation of God, however, is more than the scientist's study of his problem. We must distinguish between problem and mystery. We use the two words rather loosely and inter-

---

[3] Matthew 10:19–20.

[4] "Percy B. Shelley: A Defence of Poetry" in *Essays of British Essayists* (London, 1900), p. 165.

[5] Louis Figuier, *Vie des savants illustrés* (Paris, 1870), trans. by Barrett H. Clark in *Great Short Biographies of Modern Times* (New York, 1929), p. 713.

changeably. For instance, the performance of my TV set often exceeds my power of explanation and adjustment. And I exclaim, "This thing is a mystery to me." But the proper manipulation of the TV set is a problem which more skillful hands can solve, whereas, as Rudolf Otto observed, "the truly mysterious object, on the other hand, is beyond our apprehension and comprehension, not only because our knowledge has certain irremovable limits, but because in it we come upon something inherently 'wholly other', whose kind and character are incommensurable with our own."[1]

Suppose that after we have solved the problem of adjusting the TV set we go on to contemplate the Power that is behind television, the Power that puts into the air elements which can be harnessed to carry sound and sight through stone walls and across continents, the Power that puts into the mind of man the genius to utilize the ether waves. When we try to think behind the things we manipulate to their source and meaning, then we do confront mystery.

When we thus distinguish between problem and mystery, we begin to see the difference in function between science and religion. Science attacks the problem; religion goes beyond to confront the mystery. If disease or disaster befall us, we should use our best scientific means to discover the cause and cure. And when we think of the progress science has made, we hesitate to set limits to the problems which it can solve. One can foresee the time when cures will be found for the diseases we now consider deadly just as tuberculosis and pneumonia are no longer necessarily fatal. Many scientists now predict travel to the moon within twenty-five years; others are suggesting that man may reanimate life on dead planets. There is no foreseeable limit to man's inventive skill. But, however far man adventures, he will still say what Job and Paul said, that the judgments of God are unfathomable and his ways past finding out. He will still be reaching for the unattainable and the inexplicable.

From Wonders to Wonder

We are greater than we know and we always shall be. Science is ever pushing back frontiers but the genuine scientist is aware that

---

[1] Rudolf Otto, *The Idea of the Holy* (London, 1936), p. 28.

the more we know the greater grows the consciousness of mystery.

When Gilbert Chesterton was asked to suggest a motto for an exhibit at the Chicago Exposition of 1933, he wrote that men will never starve for want of wonders but men may starve for want of wonder. New "wonders" in the realm of physical science are being reported with such rapidity that the headlines of today's inventions and discoveries scarcely receive back-page attention in tomorrow's papers. We are getting so used to "wonders" that we are in danger of losing our capacity for wonder.

When men cease to be "lost in wonder, love, and praise," they are in spiritual peril. Hear this warning from no less a scientist than Einstein as reported in the New York *Times* in 1930: "The most beautiful and profound emotion we can experience is the mystical. It is the source of all true art and science. He to whom this emotion is a stranger, who can no longer pause to wonder and stand rapt in awe, is as good as dead; his eyes are closed. This insight into the mystery of life, coupled though it be with fear, also has given rise to religion. To know that what is impenetrable to us really exists, manifesting itself as the highest wisdom and the most radiant beauty which our dull faculties can comprehend—this knowledge, this feeling is at the center of true religiousness. In this sense, and in this sense only, I belong in the ranks of devoutly religious men."

The study of our physical sciences leaves us in possession of the truth that there is a reality beyond the reach of our senses and the range of our reason.

From the Visible to the Invisible and Eternal

It may be admitted that certain mystical moods give a power of vision into the regions which "eye hath not seen and ear hath not heard," and yet the knowledge of this fact does not necessarily give the buoyancy to our living which counteracts the down-to-earth gravity of the material. To translate this knowledge into actual and frequent experience, to put people into vital possession of supersensuous values, is the challenging task of church leaders if they are to show themselves both good "servants of Christ" and "stewards of the mysteries of God."[1]

---

[1] 1 Corinthians 4:1.

The appreciation of beyond-the-body values will not be attained by trying to discount sense enjoyment. Buddha's emphasis may have its appeal to the impoverished villagers of the Orient where life is an almost intolerable repetition of burdensome daily routine. "Delivered from the narrow bonds of sense, I go to a place of never-ending rest. Lo! I leave these things—earth, air, fire and water—to rest secure where neither birth nor death may come. Oh why should I be sorrowful! I have kept till now this sickly, crumbling body, but now I have come to the great resting place, all springs of sorrow now forever stopped."[2]

Quite in contrast to this negation of the senses was the attitude of Christ. He, too, could say on the eve of his death, "Be of good cheer, I have overcome the world."[3] But his victory might be called a triumph of spiritual athleticism, not asceticism. Jesus, the virile vigorous man of the out of doors, the joyous table companion and wedding guest, came that men "may have life, and have it abundantly."[4] Jesus did not deny the body its place in the make-up of life. The Master Teacher saw what the schools of today see—that the body can best be kept from intruding on the mind by proper exercise and attention. It would be un-Christlike, as well as foolish and futile, to attempt a return to the monastic condemnation of the physical aspects of living.

And it is not enough merely to counsel our contemporary materialistic society against laying up "treasures on earth where moth and rust consume and where thieves break through and steal."[5] Our machine-age culture is pretty firmly wedded to material possessions and comforts. And when a person is devotedly wedded to another, the union is not broken by a third person's criticism of the beloved. The disparaging remarks regarding her husband's ability which a wife overhears at a tea party do not destroy her love for him. They are more likely to break up the tea party! Similarly, the pulpit's denunciation of material interests does little to weaken the parishion-

---

[2] Quoted by Oscar Kuhns, *The Peaceful Life* (New York, 1917), p. 21.
[3] John 16:33.
[4] John 10:10.
[5] Matthew 6:19.

ers' attachment to them. It frequently serves to drive them to the more pleasing and palatable promises of the cults and churches which emphasize the psychology of success.

Yet while it is ineffectual to spend much time in disparaging the material aspects of life, it is essential to recognize that "no one can serve two masters; for either he will hate the one and love the other, or he will be devoted to the one and despise the other. You cannot serve God and mammon."[6] Those who would appropriate the values beyond the senses must give priority to the things of the spirit. As the author of the *Theologia Germanica* wisely says: "The created soul of man hath also two eyes; one has the power of seeing into eternity, the other of seeing into time and the creatures, of perceiving how they differ from each other, of giving life and needful things to the body and ordering it and governing it for the best. But these two eyes of the soul cannot both perform their work at once."

We must free ourselves from the slavery to our physical senses. It requires effort to acquire the Apostle's habit of mind that looks "not to the things that are seen but to the things that are unseen." To be sure, "the things that are seen are transient" but they are also attractive; and "the things that are unseen are eternal," but they are also elusive.[7]

And Christ tried to teach his disciples how to dwell joyously in this world while yielding sovereignty to the love of God. The Christian is to live on the streets of men "where cross the crowded ways of life"; yet as that great servant of humanity, Walter Rauschenbusch, could say, so must each healthy Christian be able to say: "In the castle of my soul is a little postern gate, whereat, when I enter, I am in the presence of God."

If we are to love God with all the soul, we must cultivate the use of the postern gate as well as the street door. We must be healthy of body and social in spirit to develop the external world. But we must be assiduous in our spiritual exercises to build up the inner man. Continued practice after a while reveals that, "though our outer nature is wasting away, our inner nature is being renewed every

---

[6] Matthew 6:24.
[7] 2 Corinthians 4:18.

day."[8] In our physical activities and social contacts we eventually cross the watershed of life and our bodily vitality begins to flow away from us. A father's powers of love, however, do not grow feebler when his limbs become infirm. The capacity for love is enlarged by exercise and there is no point of inevitable decline. The enjoyment of a great concert increases the ability to appreciate other noble harmonies. The conquest of one temptation strengthens us for our struggle with the next. In the life of the spirit all our gains are capitalized and interest is compounded. We go on from victory unto victory.

Prepared to Pray

Wherever we uncover the ruins of man's earliest civilization, we find his shrines of prayer. Man is a praying animal. The beasts of the field may lie down content after they have eaten and drunk their fill and satisfied their physical urges, but man "looks before and after and pines for what is not." Man is "such stuff as dreams are made on." And also such stuff as prayers are made by.

Why does man persist in praying and seeking for God? According to C. G. Jung, everyone's ultimate aim and strongest desire lie in developing the fullness of human existence that is called personality. This is a goal, as he points out, to be realized through the establishment of personal relations between the human personality and a Power outside itself. Man is created with hungers which his body cannot satisfy and with a reach of mind that exceeds his grasp. Man cannot integrate himself around himself.

Since man has been created with this desire to pray, are we to believe that in this law-abiding universe the Creator has made man to be fooled by false instinctive desires? Rather, we agree with Pascal that we seek God because we have already found him; that is, it is our experience of God which makes us want to know him more.

We should ever remember that the Bible interprets God as taking the initiative in his relations with man. God is not an aloof Being waiting to be discovered. Jesus taught that God is a Heavenly Father who seeks us as the father of the prodigal saw his son coming afar

---

[8] 2 Corinthians 4:16.

off and went forth to meet him. Hence, in preparing ourselves to pray, we are to make ourselves responsive to the God who is seeking us, so that we shall recognize his presence.

In praying, listening is preparatory to talking. There is a word which appears scores of times in Scripture but is seldom heard in our conversation. It is the word "hearken," which is a stronger word than "listen."

To hearken is to listen intently with faculties alert. Watch a little child playing on the floor. He talks to his dolls. He chatters to his mother. Then suddenly a strange noise at the door arrests his attention. The child halts his movements, perhaps even holds his breath. He strains to hear the next sound. Or watch a person in church sitting rather listlessly. Then something is said which arrests his attention, and he "picks up his ears," which have been lying idle beside his head. This alert listening is the attitude which prepares for prayer.

To hearken is to listen not only intently but expectantly. Expectancy alerts the faculties. Suppose a group of persons are sitting in a room. One is a mother who is expecting her son to return tonight from an army training camp. The others in the room do not know this. Who in the group would be the first to hear the car on the road or the step on the walk? The mother, of course. It makes a difference whether we listen for God expectantly or indifferently or listlessly. In praying as in all endeavor, we need what William James called "the will to believe." ". . . whoever would draw near to God must believe that he exists."[1]

Furthermore, the word "hearken" carries an added implication. It is defined as "to attend what is said for the purpose of obeying or complying." There is little use in listening for God's answers to our prayers unless we are willing to obey when we hear.

How, then, do we prepare ourselves to seek God? By remembering that he is a Father seeking us, by listening intently and expectantly and obediently for his approach.

Now let us note a second condition in finding God. Jeremiah interprets God as saying: "You will seek me and find me; when you seek me with all your heart, I will be found by you."[2]

---

[1] Hebrews 11:6.
[2] Jeremiah 29:13.

When we pray, are we really seeking God or are we seeking what he can give us? Consider a simple parable. When a father returns from a trip, his little children may gather around him, crying, "What did you bring us?" And the father enjoys watching their little chubby fingers untying the presents. He is glad to see their eagerness and happiness at what he can give them. Nevertheless, it does warm his heart if his little four-year-old climbs up and gives him a hug, crying, "Daddy, I'm glad you're home." And later, when those children are grown to college age, it would almost break the father's heart to discover that their chief thought of him concerned what he could give them.

Likewise our love for God is tested by the question of whether we seek him or his gifts. A great deal is being written about prayer today. Most writers warn against the crassness of praying for material things, but so often the petitions still remain self-centered. The questions commonly asked are along these lines: What can prayer do for my ailment? Can prayer free me from anxiety and fear? Can God help me cure this habit? What good does it do to pray for my sick child?

Such questions are all right in their time and place but they are not the kind of questions with which to begin praying—or to put first in our thought of prayer. They reveal that we are thinking more about God's gifts than about him. In Our Lord's Prayer he taught us to begin, "Our Father who art in heaven, hallowed be thy name." Our first attitude in prayer is to hearken to God, keeping our thoughts focused on him, and not looking too quickly to see what he is to do for us.

In preparing to pray, we should fasten our gaze on God until we do hallow his name and like the psalmist exclaim: "O Lord, our Lord, how majestic is thy name in all the earth! . . . I look at thy heavens, the work of thy fingers, the moon and the stars which thou hast established."[3] Keep on looking and go on with the psalmist: "I will give thanks to the Lord with my whole heart; I will tell of all thy wonderful deeds. . . . I will sing praise to thy name, O Most High."[4]

---

[3] Psalms 8:1, 3.
[4] Psalms 9: 1–2.

From Awe to Adoration

Of the godly man the First Psalm says: ". . . his delight is in the law of the Lord, and on his law he meditates day and night."[1]

His daily meditation is the cause as well as the result of his delight. Familiar in some rural communities is a colloquial expression used to describe the first stages of a romance. It is said of the young love-maker: "John is paying attention to Mary." By paying attention to the charms of the young woman, the young man begins to fall in love with her. And as his love grows he pays closer attention and then more attentions.

That this principle applies to our relationship with God is shown in the familiar invocation: "Almighty God from whom every good prayer cometh, and who pourest out on all who desire it the spirit of grace and supplication, deliver us when we draw nigh to thee from coldness of heart and wanderings of mind that with steadfast thought and kindled affection, we may worship thee in spirit and in truth, through Jesus Christ Our Lord."

But many of us find it difficult to channel our wandering minds into steadfast thought on things spiritual. We may bow our heads in prayer but our thoughts stray in reverie or run off to all sorts of secular interests. The world's increasing tempo crowds us with such a multitude of pressing and well-advertised concerns that it becomes ever harder to hold attention to the things that are invisible. With our improved means of communication and our speed of travel we get more impressions in a day than our grandfathers did in a week, but we have weakened our powers of sustained attention to things both unseen and seen. In a recent cartoon, one person asks another at a cocktail party if he has read a certain book, and the latter answers, "Not personally." Our news, our books, our opinions are "briefed" for us to save us from reading and thinking.

It was only a sidelight but an illuminating one which Whitehead gave in his assertion that religion is what a man does with his solitariness. And modern man seems to be making less and less of his solitude. He is finding it ever harder to sit still and do nothing with

---

[1] Psalms 1:2.

his body. He lights a cigarette, calls for a drink or something to eat, picks up a paper, reaches for a phone. He is as restless in his aloneness as in his activity. When moved to action, as Stephen Leacock said, man "mounts his horse and rides off in all directions." Rodin would search long for sitters if he were trying to reproduce "The Thinker." We have to school our thoughts into steadfastness. We need visible and specific aids if we are to be delivered from wandering of mind. Only by steady patient training of the mind do we gradually form channels along which our devotional energies flow.

Praying for God

For one thing, we must set our minds gazing at God. The psalmist writes: "I keep the Lord always before me."[1] When Jesus was asked to teach his disciples to pray, he gave as the first petition, "Our Father who art in heaven, hallowed be thy name." A wise commentator in expounding that first petition of the Lord's Prayer headed the section with the words "Praying for God." It may seem absurd to speak of praying for God. Does the all-powerful God need our prayers? Yes, if he is to do what he desires to do with us and for us. Just as an earthly father wishes and waits for the co-operation of his children in order to do certain things, so Our Heavenly Father wishes and waits for a right spirit in us. And the first phase of a right spirit is setting our wills to desire God's welfare.

We open the windows of our minds and the doors of our wills to the glorious and spacious thoughts of God. We inhale the pure air of the eternal. We stretch our imaginations to picture the Creator of the universe who is from everlasting to everlasting.

If we can keep looking at God's majesty and power, our wonder deepens into awe. Dr. John Casteel cites a distinguished chemist who became impressed by the wonder of water. He was not thinking of the beauty of water as seen in the blue depths of a mountain lake or tumbling over the stones in a sparkling waterfall or rolling majestically against the headlands of the sea. The chemist had in mind those qualities of water which make it so serviceable: the quality of water which makes it evaporate and return as rainfall; the quality

---

[1] Psalms 16:8.

which makes it able to produce horsepower as steam; the quality which makes it expand when frozen so that ice does not settle to the bottom of our lakes and rivers and turn the earth into a deep freeze; the quality of water which makes weight unable to compress it and thus enables ships to float.[2] The glory of the commonplace as well as the grandeur of the spectacular evoke wonder and awe.

And what does God like? Of what do we think when we repeat the petition, "Thy kingdom come, thy will be done on earth as it is in heaven"? Our thoughts should be sufficiently sweeping to envision God's rule spreading over the earth, replacing the rule of unrighteous holders of power, removing the barriers to peace, cleansing the world of vice and violence. Also our thoughts should be sufficiently searching to ask what God's rule would mean in our own lives. Are we really saying, "Not my will but thine be done"?

Too many of us race through the Lord's Prayer without stopping to ask ourselves how much the coming of God's kingdom would change our own lives. If we were to pause and ponder what we might have to give up to take God's rule in, it might stop our petition. Coleridge points the truth in *The Rime of the Ancient Mariner:*

> *I looked to heaven, and tried to pray;*
> *But or ever a prayer had gusht,*
> *A wicked whisper came, and made*
> *My heart as dry as dust.*

The prayer, "Thy will be done," is an offering quite as truly as a petition, for the kingdom of God is in our midst, waiting to come into our lives whenever we open our minds and surrender our spirits. Before we ask God for what we want, let us fasten our thoughts on God to find out what he wants. Prayer has been likened to the boat hook which the boatman uses to pull his craft to the anchoring place. The boatman does not pull the shore to the boat. So in prayer we should try to draw ourselves to God and not pull God down to us.

[2] John Casteel, *The Rediscovery of Prayer* (New York, 1955), p. 28.

Where God Comes Closest

But the Christian petitioner does not have to pull God down to himself. He can feel that God is coming of his own accord. Plato and Aristotle among the pre-Christian Greeks represented God as the Absolute and changeless Good, pursued and longed for by the soul. The earlier Old Testament prophets pictured the Lord as the High and Holy One to whom suppliants brought their sacrificial offerings. But Jesus revealed God as the pursuer and man as the pursued.

Some of us have to confess our difficulty in holding our thoughts very long and steadfastly on God as Absolute Good or Ultimate Value. Also we cannot testify that the awe aroused by nature's wonders kindles very warm affections in our hearts for God as First Cause. To repeat "God is Love," "God is Truth," does have some value. Such concepts do color our thoughts. But they are too impersonal.

Some pages of this book were written at Chamonix under the shadow of Mont Blanc. The majesty of that massive mountain cast a spell over my spirit. Passengers being carried in cable cars up to the lower adjoining peaks were dwarfed to the appearance of dark dots against the snow. From Aiguille du Midi, three thousand feet below Mont Blanc's summit, one can look down into France, Italy, and Switzerland. Even national boundaries seem subordinated to insignificant fences by God's great stone walls. Gazing at the snow of Mont Blanc, I could understand the mood of the psalmist: "I lift up my eyes to the hills. From whence does my help come? My help comes from the Lord, who made heaven and earth."[1] The mountains manifest the eternal power of the Creator which makes man's troubles seem transient and trivial.

And yet, though the mountains inspire awe, they seem so aloof, so indifferent to man. They stand there so heedless as climbers fall from their cold and rocky sides. The God of nature has no arms.

I had come to Mont Blanc fresh from a visit to Avila where St. Teresa by her radiance of spirit had reformed and renewed the religious and monastic life of Spain. The glow of her faith gave light

---

[1] Psalms 121:1-2.

to drab lives and darkened minds and in that light the faithful felt the love and compassion of God. Personality has a power of spiritual transmission not possessed by mountains. Life comes from life. The Word must become flesh and dwell among us. This was the realization that came to men supremely in the person of Jesus Christ.

"God is a spirit and those who worship him must worship in spirit and truth."[2] And when we find it hard to visualize the divine Spirit, we remember the words of Jesus: "He who has seen me has seen the Father."[3] Many of us can best make God real by looking at Jesus Christ, for in the personality of Jesus we see the character and purpose of God.

In cultivating the presence of God, Protestants have counted too much on the human ear, too little on the eye. We must remember that the eye is the pope of the senses. Send a class of students into a room for three minutes, asking them to make mental note of all the features and phenomena in the room. When they come out to compile the list of things noted, see how many put down the features observed by the eye and how many fail to mention perhaps the sound of a piano wafted in from an adjoining room or a slight odor pervading the atmosphere. Yet despite the predominance of eye sensations, Protestants have been neglecting visual aids to prayer and worship. Most of us would feel God more real if we prayed with our eyes on a worthy likeness of Christ. We close our eyes in prayer to shut out the world but so often we shut our minds into self-centered or scattered vagaries.

The Roman Catholic Church attempts to make God's love personal and appealing through the representation of "Mary the Mother of God" and the various saints. We do not need the use of such intermediaries if we fix our eyes and thoughts on the living Christ himself. While visible figures and symbols of Christ in our prayer rooms or on our altars aid the imagination, we should go on to form pictures of him in our minds. We can picture him sitting on the hillside teaching his disciples, or stooping to touch the eyes of the blind, or standing calmly before Pilate, or sitting with his friends at the Last

---

[2] John 4:24.
[3] John 14:9.

Supper. Vital Christian prayer can hardly be sustained without Bible reading—a point overlooked by many current books on prayer.

A very discerning woman wrote a book some years ago under the title, *I Follow the Road*. She was steeped in literature and interested in the fine arts. Perhaps her artistic taste shaped her patterns of thought, for this is what she did. With a little coterie of friends she chose for their weekly group meditations certain scenes from Christ's life which had a special bearing on some weaknesses of the members. For instance, one person in the group was overtalkative. Hence they would sit and ponder the scene of Christ standing silent before Pilate while the babel of voices could be heard outside calling for his crucifixion. Or when a member was present who was intellectually proud and looked down on the less learned, the group would meditate on the scene wherein Jesus set a little child in the midst of the crowd and said, "Whoever humbles himself like this child, he is the greatest in the kingdom of heaven."[4]

Lost in Wonder, Love, and Praise

If our thought of God is to advance from meditation to love, we must safeguard prayer from mushing down into mere subjectivity. Here vocal praying helps. To be sure, we can be in the spirit of prayer without uttering words or bowing heads or bending knees. Du Maurier makes l'Endormi say of Trilby's singing: "To sing like that is to pray and thinking is praying very often (don't you think so?), and so is being ashamed when one has done a mean thing, and grateful when it is a fine day. . . . Prayers without words are the best."

But we must beware not to carry such reasoning too far. While it is true that, "If I speak in the tongues of men and of angels, but have not love, I am a noisy gong or a clanging cymbal,"[1] it is also true that love needs words to keep the music and romance in it, as many a husband and wife would do well to remember.

In our blaring, raucous, chattering world, silence is golden. And to sit in silence with one's beloved is often a form of deep communion. But if love is never given expression in words, the golden silence

---

[4] Matthew 18:4. Cf. Anne Payson, *I Follow the Road* (New York, 1934).
[1] 1 Corinthians 13:1.

can become leaden. Likewise in our love of God we need to voice our devotion, our praise, our gratitude. "For man believes with his heart and so is justified and he confesses with his lips and so is saved."[2] When we mention our sin aloud, we set it more clearly before the conscience. When we put our blessings into spoken words, we kindle our affection for God. The psalmist saw the need of voicing our feelings when he prayed, "O Lord, open thou my lips, and my mouth shall show forth thy praise."[3] The Methodist movement owes almost as much to Charles Wesley for his hymns as to John Wesley for his organizing genius. Theology without hymnology would create a cold and sterile church.

Actions as well as words serve as aids in our devotional life. The James-Lange law is relevant to religious as well as romantic love. The devoted husband kisses his wife because he loves her and his kiss increases his love. Our emotions are very closely connected with the appropriate gestures which have become associated with them. Kneeling does tend to put us in a prayerful mood. St. Ignatius gave very careful and exact directions for the bodily behavior of those going through spiritual exercises.

St. Teresa advised her nuns to "get themselves some company when first they go to prayer." The novice in prayer needs the aid of corporate worship in opening channels of devotion and the veteran devotee needs the contagion of fellow worshipers to keep his love warm and his faith vital. Evelyn Underhill asserts that in the long run we come closer to God through common worship than through closet worship. While our most intimate and real experiences of God's presence often seem to come in our aloneness, nevertheless the nature of religion is such that it needs to be nurtured by togetherness in order to preserve the cultivation of private devotion.

Corporate worship calls us back to the divine source of love as life force. It sets us in the continuity of a historic movement and makes us feel that we are directing our steps in paths "where the saints have trod." It sustains our spirits by the shoulder-to-shoulder touch with fellow seekers who, like ourselves, may often falter but who are kept

---

[2] Romans 10:10.
[3] Psalms 51:15.

from utterly falling by comradeship in Christ. When we forget ourselves in the fellowship of a worshiping congregation, focus our eyes and thoughts on the symbols of God's love, join in liturgies and hymns hallowed by tradition and testing, we tend to become "lost in wonder, love, and praise."

William James described his religious feeling as somewhat like a tune singing in the back of his mind. In corporate worship that tune in the back of our minds breaks forth from our lips and our love of God rises toward adoration. Our awareness of divine love wells up in hymns like this:

> *For the beauty of the earth,*
> *For the glory of the skies,*
> *For the love which from our birth,*
> *Over and around us lies:*
> *Lord of all, to Thee we raise*
> *This our hymn of grateful praise.*

In worship the divine love becomes more vividly personal than in nature. The Creator is seen as the God who "so loved the world that he gave his only Son, that whoever believes in him should not perish but have eternal life."[4]

The Son of God is seen entering the world in the beauty of Bethlehem. The purity of his life, the loftiness of his spirit, the unsearchable riches of his mind, the inexhaustible range of his love, remain the unmatched miracle of the ages, and worshipers are moved to sing, "O come, let us adore him, Christ the Lord."

The gentleness of Jesus was blended with such gianthood of strength that the longer we ponder him the more we come under the spell of his power. That "strange man on the cross" rules from his rude throne with a sway unapproached by any Caesar with his scepter. Political rulers may scorn the principles of Jesus as impracticable and deride him as a dreamer, but out of the wreckage of failures and wars increasing hosts of the wise wake up to the eternal rightness of Jesus and sing: "Lead on, O King Eternal."

---

[4] John 3:16.

The rulership of Christ reaches into those inner realms which physical power, however amazingly developed, cannot penetrate. The jet plane may carry the sorrowing passenger to the bedside of a dying loved one, but it has no power to comfort a breaking heart. The Great Physician has. Christ can "pluck from the breast the rooted sorrow" and "break the power of cancelled sin." Christ can give mastery in the face of immovable pain and frustration, when, "having done all, we stand" and keep standing. Christ convinces us of a divine love from which nothing can separate us. "Who shall separate us from the love of Christ? Shall tribulation, or distress, or persecution, or famine, or nakedness, or peril, or sword? . . . No, in all these things we are more than conquerors through him who loved us."[5]

In Christ we see the love of God flowing as a life-giving spring from the heart of the Eternal:

> Jesus, Thou Joy of loving hearts,
> Thou Fount of life, Thou Light of men.
> From the best bliss that earth imparts
> We turn unfilled to Thee again.

And when we behold Christ on the cross, praying for his crucifiers, we hear love's last word, and cry with Isaac Watts:

> Were the whole realm of nature mine,
> That were a present far too small.
> Love so amazing, so divine,
> Demands my soul, my life, my all.

God's love for us puts song in our hearts and, when we respond to his love by letting ourselves go in hymns of praise, thanksgiving, and adoration, we are lifted to the plane where we comprehend what it is to love the Lord with all the soul.

In Malott's version of the Lord's Prayer, which has become so popular, the voice begins softly, then sinks almost to a whisper, and finally rises to a crescendo in the words, "For thine is the Kingdom and the Power and the Glory, Forever and ever, Amen." Those clos-

---

[5] Romans 8:35, 37.

ing climactic words were not recorded as given by Jesus in his version of the prayer. Reliable commentators believe that they were added by the early Christians as a spontaneous doxology. Having looked to God the Father in heaven, having prayed for his will to be done, having felt the sustenance of his daily bread and the deliverance from evil through his forgiving grace, those early followers of Christ burst into an ascription of praise and joyous adoration.

The Know-Why and the Know-How

The young man who falls in love with a young woman does not thereby fully fit himself to be a good husband. He may lose his heart to his beloved, but he must use his head if he is to make his love lasting and satisfying.

And he usually does employ about all the resources of his mind. He tries to learn all he can about the object of his love. He seeks to see her as often as possible. He reads and rereads her letters. He uses his imagination to anticipate her desires. He talks about her to other people. In college I roomed with a student who fell in love. I remember that night after night his falling in love kept me from falling asleep. In short, true love involves every resource of the mind.

So is it in our relation with God. It does not take a great mind to love God, but it takes all the mind we have. The gospel of Christ is so simple that little children and illiterate yokels can respond to it, but whoever loves God wants to learn all he can about him. Lack of study, therefore, indicates lack of love.

We are born with a desire to know about the world around us. A normal child is as full of questions as a porcupine is full of quills. He is ever letting fly his "hows" and "whats" and "whys"!

A child's questions fly up to include God as naturally as smoke rises from the ground. "Who is God?" "Where does God live?" "Where do we go when we die?" Such queries come normally from the lips of children. They seldom receive serious or helpful answers, partly because parents do not know how to reply and partly because the adults think the children are too young to understand. The fail-

WITH ALL YOUR MIND   81

ure to encourage children's questing for God tends to make them spiritual orphans.

As the mind matures, the search for spiritual meanings widens and deepens. We look at man and, with Shakespeare, we exclaim: "What a piece of work is a man! how noble in reason! how infinite in faculty! in form and moving how express and admirable! in action how like an angel! in apprehension how like a god!" We see man longing for truth and beauty, for justice and mercy, and we ask whence come these ideals. We see that men everywhere in all ages have been building shrines and altars for what they call worship, and that worship has inspired the most magnificent architecture, the noblest art, the richest music, and the sturdiest characters. If we are mentally alert, we long to know about the source of this pervasive religious faith.

As Henry Van Dusen puts it, religious interest rises out of a twofold desire: desire for light on the mystery of things, and desire for power for the mastery of things. Our power-minded, profit-seeking, utilitarian age has been putting emphasis on the quest for power rather than meaning. Books of the "how to" variety have been pouring from the press. The tendency has tinctured religion. Prayer has been presented as a means of mastering fear and anxiety, as a way to social acceptance and financial success. God has been treated as a servant of our desires and not as the sovereign of our allegiance and devotion.

While such presentations have been seeking popularity by posing as the bulwark against communism, they have surrendered to the spirit of Karl Marx, who asked impatiently, Why bother to interpret the world when the point is to change it? But Roger Hazleton pertinently comments in reply to Marx: "Revolution is usually the last resort of those who have not the patience needed for reflection; and the way in which we change the world depends directly upon the way in which we interpret it."[1] And we might say both to the communist revolutionaries and to the conservative counterrevolutionaries that the time has come for stressing the "know-why" as well as the "know-how."

---

[1] Roger Hazleton, *Renewing the Mind* (New York, 1949), p. 9.

In the spring of 1955 was held a conference of foreign students now attending American universities. Representatives of various foreign governments spoke of their gratitude to America for what she was doing for their students. A government spokesman for Pakistan said that his country was deeply indebted to the United States for giving the students the "know-how," but he added that he was not sure she was giving them the "know-what."

College professors have suggested to college preachers that the students needed more sermons of a philosophical nature than the psychological type. Psychology is popular because we are all interested in taking ourselves apart and finding new sources of self-help. But the greater need of the students is for a philosophy of life which gives meaning and wholeness.

The student mind is both at sea and at bay. The kaleidoscopic changes and intercontinental contacts have carried youth out from the old moorings and landmarks. It is difficult to get one's bearings. So many young people are living on short-term contracts with life. If H. G. Wells before his death thought the human mind had reached the end of its tether, one wonders what he would think now.

The findings of science are expanding with dizzying speed. Books are written on "The Fabulous Future." Yet, even before space travel was opened by the sputniks, Joseph Wood Krutch was asserting that the present generation is less sure of what is ahead than was any of its predecessors. The reason for such an arresting statement is that man now has the power to commit race suicide. No matter how bad men were in the past, they had neither the power nor the nearness to their neighbors to kill them off. Now with our nuclear weapons we have the power and with our jet planes and guided missiles we have the proximity.[2]

The awareness of this danger is driving thoughtful minds to a new intensity and dimension of search for light on the mystery of things and for power to master things. This deepened concern could prove the matrix of a genuine spiritual revival if properly directed and extended.

---

[2] Cf. J. W. Krutch, *The Measure of Man* (New York, 1953).

Can We See Light?

In contrast to our disordered society we can and should see and stress the divine orderliness. A bird's-eye view of the human scene reveals men and nations going around in vicious circles of recurring iniquities, but the birds that view such human chaos are themselves guided through the trackless air on their unerring migrations. Radio and television may shake our faith with the tragic news of accumulating disasters, but these inventions are themselves revelations of "something far more deeply interfused, whose dwelling is the light of setting suns, and the round ocean, and the living air." When society seems so senseless in its sinfulness, we can look at the fidelities of nature and feel with Einstein a "profound reverence for the rationality made manifest in existence."[1]

We cannot explain the physical creation without a First Cause. Some Power there must be which started the stars spinning through space and holds them in their courses. Some great Organizer must have arranged the seasons and ordered the speed of light and sound. Some great Originator there must be that gives rise to the ideals and hopes of human hearts, for water does not rise above its source. Some ultimate values there must be by which the things we prize are measured. The more society is shaken, the more we realize the unshakable foundations of the universe.

And this seeking for light on the mystery is a manifestation of our love of God. God, if there be a God, must be ultimate truth. Hence the scientist in his love and search for truth is pursuing the love of God. God, if there be a God, must be ultimate beauty. Hence the artist in his pursuit of the beautiful is manifesting the love of God. God, if there be a God, must be ultimate goodness. Hence, our efforts to satisfy the promptings of conscience are a phase of love for God. Even though we may not feel ourselves engaged in a religious exercise, yet this seeking for ultimate values demonstrates our love

---

[1] Albert Einstein, "Science and Religion." Address at Conference on Science, Philosophy, and Religion, held at Columbia University, September 9, 10, 11, 1940.

of God, "for God is at work in you, both to will and to work for his good pleasure."[2]

Can We Find Purpose?

Yet the contemplation of God as First Cause or as Ultimate Value is a pretty pale form of love. Experiences come which drive the mind below the level of mere intellectual curiosity. Some years ago, in a time of deep sorrow, we visited the lovely old city of Charleston, South Carolina. We found there a measure of comfort. The restless yet regular tides of the sea suggested the eternal amid the changing. The beautiful magnolia gardens reminded us of life rising out of death. But our comfort came from the double revelation of God through nature and human nature. The beauty in the heart of man which helped him to work with God in creating those gardens; the sense of the eternal which had inspired men to build those beautiful churches; the sympathy of friends who entered into our sorrow—all these served to lift the clouds of our depression and reveal horizons beyond the reach of death.

When we look deeply at human nature as well as at nature, we discern indications of divine purpose amid the disorder. To be sure, two world wars within living memory have shattered the easy concepts of progress with which the present century began. We could apostrophize the goddess of progress with the words applied to liberty in the French Revolution: "O Progress, what crimes have been committed in thy name." But take the long view. From the mud of the cave man up to the majesty of the Taj Mahal and the Chartres Cathedral; from the growls of the savage in his war dance to the singing of the Hallelujah Chorus in a church—these are gradations upward which indicate direction and purpose. With Arnold Toynbee we feel justified in tracing some patterns of purpose in history.

And when we turn from the secular realm to Scripture, we observe the writers interpreting the purpose of God as redemptive. The prophet Isaiah pictures God as measuring the "waters in the hollow of his hand" and holding the nations "like a drop from a bucket."[1] And then in the same chapter Isaiah says, "He will feed his flock like

---

[2] Philippians 2:13.
[1] Isaiah 40:12, 15.

a shepherd, he will gather the lambs in his arms." And in "the full-ness of time" came Jesus of Nazareth.

When we enter a movie while a picture is in progress, we not only follow the action but we try to reconstruct in our imagination what happened before we came in. Thus we "get the hang of the story." Similarly, in the dramatic life of Jesus, his biographers came on the stage after he had begun his ministry. They had not been eye-witnesses at Bethlehem, and they had to reconstruct the events of his birth. Hence the accounts of the nativity were their inspired inter-pretations of what happened, based on the stories which were afloat.

And the stories make us feel that the Almighty God had stooped to our weakness and become incarnate in a babe born in a manger. The child grew, tempted in all points as we are, and yet without sin. His matchless purity and invincible love became the lasting miracles of the ages. He manifested such wisdom in his words and such power in his works that his followers became convinced that he is "the Christ, the Son of the living God."[2]

The more the mind ponders the person of Jesus Christ, the more it feels that he sheds light on the mystery of things. In his face we behold the glory of God. In his character and work we see the pur-pose of God. In his redemptive mission we comprehend the "theology of crisis" as a corrective to the "theology of progress."

Personality is the highest form of creation we know. And Jesus of Nazareth is the noblest personality we have seen or can imagine. Hence we conclude that God the All-Highest must be like Christ. And in Christ's brief life is to be discerned the design of the divine intention.

We do not turn to Jesus' words for scientific knowledge or eco-nomic blueprints. Some critics have asserted that all of Jesus' sayings can be paralleled in pre-Christian sources. Granted that many of the basic ideas enunciated by Jesus can be found embedded in ear-lier writings, nevertheless he put them in such form and force that he made them live. The fundamental principle of the Golden Rule is older than Christ, but he gave it life. Pious counsels of kindness have been given from the dawn of history, but Jesus created the

---

[2] Matthew 16:16.

figure of a Good Samaritan who made the concept of kindness and neighborliness a living, breathing, unforgettable force.

For the Greek, religion was man's climb upward to the realm of the divine. For the Christian, the gospel was the drama of God's descent to man.

The wisdom of the East which preceded Christ compares with his as starlight with sunlight. Stars with all their beauty cannot make the grass to grow or the bodies of men to glow with health. It takes sunlight to give life. Christ had that power. "In him was life, and the life was the light of men . . . To all who received him, who believed in his name, he gave power to become children of God."[3]

Hence, through Christ we seek God with all the mind to find both the "Know-Why" and the "Know-How" of love and life.

When Is the Mind Whole?

While we are frightened by the swift development of destructive weapons, we also recognize the amazing advances in the healing art. We have removed the terrors from many diseases which our forefathers considered fatal. We have lengthened the span of life. More people are alive at sixty than ever before, and what is even more interesting, they are more alive at sixty!

And now one of the most significant and promising aspects in the health situation is the alliance between medicine and religion. Psychosomatic medicine has become a recognized field of practice. Clinics are multiplying. Competent physicians are loath to set limits to the healing potency of spiritual attitudes. And intelligent pastors seek the co-operation of doctors in their confessionals.

But in all the current talk about mental health, what does the expression suggest? Commonly it connotes freedom from anxiety and neurosis. But one wonders whether this modern concept of mental health quite represents all that the Great Physician considered essential to the healthy mind. Listeners were impressed and amazed at the qualities of Jesus' mind. When he taught his Galilean neighbors, they exclaimed, "Where did this man get this wisdom and these mighty works? Is not this the carpenter's son? Is not his mother

---

[3] John 1:4, 12.

called Mary? . . . Where then did this man get all this?"[1] It was the fullness, the range, the power of Jesus' mind, rather than its peace and calm, which astonished his first hearers.

And while Jesus did seek to allay needless fears and weakening anxieties, his major emphasis seemed to be to alert and enlarge the thinking of his countrymen rather than to dispense tranquilizers. "Do not think," he said, "that I have come to bring peace on earth; I have not come to bring peace, but a sword."[2] Jesus came to develop wholeness of mind, and the attainment of that often involves tension.

We need to distinguish between devilish restlessness and divine discontent. The former disrupts our peace of mind and leaves life at loose ends; the latter may temporarily disturb our peace of mind but it leads to larger and richer living. There are desires which drive us on feverishly only to leave us in frustration. There are ambitions which keep us climbing toward the longed-for summit of success only to leave us buried in an avalanche of freezing regrets. One of the great services of religious faith is to help us sift our incentives and choose what Lowell called our "golden spurs."

Much as I value the scholarship of the Revised Standard Version of the Bible, I wonder if the translators are correct in so consistently changing the word "whole" as it appears in the King James Version to the word "well." I cannot but feel that the word "whole" in many situations connotes what was in the mind of Jesus better than does the word "well," as we use it. When we speak of being well, we mean that we are free from any known physical ailment. When we say that a mental patient has been made well, do we not mean that he has been freed from his haunting fears and disordered thoughts? But does this mean that his mind has attained the wholeness desired by the Christ?

I think of a man who is about the most perfect physical specimen one can imagine. He eats what he pleases, goes where he pleases, does what he pleases. He has no disturbing complexes. He is regarded in his social circles as rather a witty conversationalist. But he is narrow in his social outlooks, rigidly opinionated in his political views, bitterly biased in his racial attitudes. He passes for a "well"

[1] Matthew 13:54–56.
[2] Matthew 10:34.

person but he is certainly not whole-minded as measured by Christ's standards. He is simply self-contained in too small a container! And what he needs is to have his mind stretched even at the cost of some tensions. He should be widened in vision and mellowed in sympathy. The shell of his selfhood needs to be broken open by the surging life force of the divine Spirit.

"It is significant that psychologists such as C. G. Jung and Fritz Künkel have recognized a deeper role for psychotherapy than it has hitherto acknowledged. Where it has been content until recently to devote itself to the salvaging of the mentally sick, it is now beginning to sense a deeper function: that of assisting those who already possess a mediocre adjustment but who are sick unto life and are reaching out for more creative levels, levels of greater abandonment, of more effective freedom. In approaching this field they are at once faced with the spiritual problem."[3]

And how does Christ help us to have a whole mind? For one thing, he would have us *see more of life*. Recall the day he set a little child in the midst of some grownups and said, ". . . unless you turn and become like children, you will never enter the kingdom of heaven."[4] Picture to yourself that little child as he stood there, his big round eyes trying to take it all in, looking at the crowd and the Christ. And remember, a little child takes in far more than we realize. If the rate at which a child receives new ideas up to the age of six years were to continue at the same speed until the age of sixty, what full rich minds we would achieve. But after a while the pace of perception slackens, the vision may become dulled by indifference or narrowed by prejudice or even blinded by hate. And the child's world of dreams and hopes all too often shrinks, as Hermann Hagedorn puts it, into a world "where men with blinded eyes and hobbled feet grope down a narrow gorge and call it life."

If we would let Christ make us whole, he would help us to see more. When I walk through a garden with a real lover of gardens, I am put to shame by the meagerness of my observation in comparison with her rich perception. Christ would have us see more species of flowers and birds. But he wants us to see something still more. Recall

[3] Douglas V. Steere, *Prayer and Worship* (New York, 1938), p. 5.
[4] Matthew 18:3.

how Jesus tried to ease the anxieties and tensions of his listeners by telling them to consider the fowls of the air. He wanted his worried hearers to note the carefree joy of the birds. Those birds were singing their hearts out because they were content to be fulfilling their God-given natures. We human beings eat our hearts out with worry because we are not content to fulfill our natures but are greedily trying to fill our nests. Christ would have us learn from nature to fulfill ourselves and not become anxious and "fed up" trying to fill ourselves.

In cities especially we are so preoccupied with ideas and emotions that many a highly educated adult never looks at an object except to use it. A group goes to the opera. The members of the party sit in the same box. One of them is there hoping to be seen by his fellow box holders. Another goes because he thinks opera going improves his general culture. Another is present in order to be able to discuss the production at a forthcoming dinner party, and another feels the need of relaxation and thinks music will be good for his health. But one of the group goes solely to enjoy the music. She has no secondary purpose. She forgets herself, she enters into the spirit of the opera, she allows herself to fall in love with the music. Beauty is a realm to which one must give himself whole-mindedly in order to appreciate it fully.

And Christ would lead us toward wholeness of mind by seeing more in human nature. In the elbowing crowds of the street, individuals do not look very attractive to us, pushing, rushing, scrambling for seats in busses and honking for places on the highway. Also people fall into such quarrelsome moods. They divide into classes according to economic or racial or national interests.

We do well to hear the words of Franz Werfel: the world has forgotten in its preoccupation with Left and Right that there is an Above and Below. It is this divine dimension of Above and Below to which Christ would open our eyes. There is a higher nature within man which is struggling upward toward ideals and hopes. There is a Higher Power, not ourselves, that makes for righteousness. And instead of thinking ever about men as "Left" or "Right" according to political attitudes, we should lift our eyes to see the spiritual division between "Above" and "Below."

The World Council of Churches met at Evanston in 1954. During the second week of its session it did consider the questions of leftness and rightness, the problems of race and labor, of war and peace. But during the first week the assembled church leaders pondered the general theme of the conference, which was, "Christ, the Hope of the World." They studied the implications of the biblical promises of Christ's return. Is it to be gradual or cataclysmic? Reporters chided the churchmen for their dry discussions of theology which had no news value. But such criticism overlooked the fact that the best minds of the church are trying to arouse people to the greatness of our gospel. In our efforts to make religion popular we have tended to bring it so much down to earth, as we say, that it now needs to be brought up to God.

Other thoughtful persons besides church leaders recognize the need to recover the wholeness of life's outlook. Recently Brooks Atkinson, the distinguished drama critic, made a plea for another play by Thornton Wilder in order that the reading public and theatergoers might have their minds stretched to ponder some great themes of living. Mr. Atkinson reminded us that in Thornton Wilder's play, *Our Town*, a letter was delivered at a little New Hampshire village with this address on the envelope: "Grover's Corners, New Hampshire, the U.S.A., continent of North America, Western Hemisphere, the Earth, the Solar System, the Mind of God." As I remember, at that point in the play a lad leaning out of the window heard the long address read by the postmaster and, wide-eyed with wonder, he exclaimed, "Well, what do you know? What do you know?" Yes, such an address does stretch our minds with wonder. And that is what we need to lift us out of our littleness.

Little Glimpses or Whole Views?

Professor Paul Hoon writes of seeing a psychological test given to a group of young people. It called for quick, off-the-cuff answers. One question was, "Do you think God understands radar?" All answered no! They looked upon God as a Being whom science had left behind. Such immature views are all too typical of contemporary youth, even of churchmen.

We have given to spiritual concerns only a fraction of the study which we accord to material interests. While many public-school educators recognize the importance of religion to the point of providing released time for its study, the achievements in this line are very partial and unsatisfactory.

Even in our churches religious education is regarded by most members as something which is supposed to stop at the teen age. Very little efficiently led Bible study is being conducted in our conventional churches and all too many contemporary sermons lack educational content. Preachers with social passion flog the wills of their parishioners but do not feed their minds. Other pulpits, in the effort to be popular, specialize on the profits to be derived from faith and prayer but they give mental tranquilizers rather than stimulants to study. It is one thing to say to a congregation, "Have faith"; it is another thing to help people to "have a faith." To have faith is an attitude of mind, a will to believe, as William James called it. To have a faith is to have a content of mind. We need both, but it is the second which is running short in current religion.

The late historian, James Truslow Adams, asserted that the greatest contribution which America has made to the world is the American dream. But many a citizen would be hard put if he were asked to define our national dream. This lack of reasoned conviction to sustain our American faith led to some tragic results in the recent Korean fighting. Our Department of Defense discovered belatedly that the defections from the American to the Red Chinese ranks were due not so much to the cleverness of the communist brainwashing as to the emptiness of the American soldiers' brains. The boys we had sent to fight in our forces were not trained in the teachings of our civic or religious faith. The building of our morale requires more than snappy pep talks and impassioned pulpit pleas to "have faith."

There has never been a genuine revival of religion in Protestantism which has not been accompanied and nurtured by a revival of Bible study. The current popular interest in religion will evaporate in sentimentalism and commercialism unless the Christian church is seriously awakened to restudy the Bible, the charter of its salvation. This will not be accomplished by authoritarian Bibliolatry. The scriptural revelation must be presented in ways which carry con-

viction to free minds. Church and community programs of adult
education need to give generous place to religious instruction. Only
a teaching church is a true church. The American pulpit needs more
expository preaching. To copy the continental patterns of pulpit exposition would hardly hold the interest of American congregations.
But gripping sermons can start on the sidewalk level where men are
living and then lead their thought into the biblical uplands of the
soul where men are "transformed by the renewing of the mind."

The Protestant church rightly boasts that the Reformation under
Luther gave us the open Bible. But are we keeping the Bible open?
To be sure, the Bible is still the world's best seller, but in many homes
the Bible is kept as a sort of amulet, an unread "Good Book," cherished in sentimental, if not superstitious, spirit. Many a devout person has certain favorite passages and is familiar with several parables
and biblical stories, and yet he may lack knowledge of the Bible as
the long panoramic unfolding revelation of God's love.

If we are to love God with all the mind, we need more than favorite verses depicting his goodness. Yes, and more than the memory
of special occasions wherein God has been good to us. Special
providences are not an adequate foundation for an abiding love of
God. After the deliverance of the British troops from the trap of
Dunkirk, sermons were delivered in American pulpits attempting
to prove that God is good because he preserved a calm sea for the
English boats. But what would such preachers say about God's goodness at Singapore some months later when overhanging clouds per-
mitted Japanese aircraft to approach undetected within destroying
distance of British warships?

An American traveler wired his home church a handsome check
because of his gratitude to God for his goodness. He had planned to
take a plane in the South Pacific. At the last minute his plans were
changed and his passage was canceled. The plane went down and
all lives were lost. The American churchman interpreted his escape
from death as a mark of God's love. His gratitude and generosity
were commendable. But second thought should raise the question,
How far can such events be interpreted as evidence of divine love?
What about God's attitude toward the passengers whose lives were
lost?

If we are to comprehend God's love for his children, we need longer and more comprehensive perspective, deeper and more sympathetic study. At this point biblical revelation helps to supplement and correct personal experience. In the Bible we follow a people dug out of obscurity in the dim misty morning of the patriarchs, Abraham, Isaac, and Jacob; we see them tested in the hardships of Egyptian slavery, led forth in a mighty exodus under Moses, welded into a nation by Saul and David, burdened and divided by the sons of Solomon, scattered in the adversities of exile, yet held together by a deathless hope kept alive by prophets of God, until in the "fullness of time" there appeared Jesus of Nazareth, whom now some six hundred millions believe to be the One who is the key by which all that preceded him can be interpreted.

From the birth of conscience in Eden to the birth of a nation in Jerusalem to the birth of a Savior in Bethlehem to the birth of a church at Pentecost, so runs the divine drama of redemption. Thus on the horizon of history is limned the long upward striving of the human spirit. The generations are linked together by faith. The old men dream their dreams and the young men catch their visions and carry on their ideals toward further goals. And out of all the disappointments and delays, the sins and setbacks of history, the divine purpose is portrayed as a kind of relay race run by those who are "looking unto Jesus the pioneer and perfecter of our faith."[1]

When we study the Bible, we need a better understanding of its subjective element as well as its historical content. We should remember Richard Niebuhr's distinction between "external history" and "inner history."[2] The case history of a hospital patient as kept by the doctors and nurses is very different from the autobiographical experience of the sick patient as he climbs back up the road to health. Yet both are real and both are history.

Case histories cannot be written of those experiences wherein prophets exclaim, "The Word of the Lord came to me." That exaltation in which Isaiah "saw the Lord sitting upon a throne, high and

---

[1] Hebrews 12:2.

[2] Richard Niebuhr, *The Meaning of Revelation* (New York, 1941), Chap. 2.

lifted up,"[3] was an experience which no reporter could photograph and no anatomist dissect. The approach to understanding revelation, therefore, is by way of preparing the mood which can receive it. When we think of the Bible as a record of history, it becomes an object of study. When we view it as a description of the ways by which divine revelation is received, it becomes a means of study. While the Bible is both an object and a means of study, it is the latter which currently needs the more emphasis. Instead of spending so much time searching for keys to the Scriptures, we might well spend more effort in using the Scriptures as keys for unlocking the secrets of progressive revelation. We should look *with* the seers even more than *at* them.

Portions of the Bible are external history, written by observers and hence subject to study and interpretation as case history. But other parts are inner history and can be apprehended only by participation. Thus in Deuteronomy we read codes of law which are objects of historic interest, adapted to a certain stage of social development. And then in their midst we come upon a line like this: "The eternal God is your dwelling place, and underneath are the everlasting arms."[4] In the spirit of Browning's words, "We musicians know," we can say to a statement like that, "We sufferers know." To those who have lived deeply such words speak with an authority derived from experience.

When we abide in the words of the spiritual seers until their words abide in us, then are we truly their disciples, able to catch the flash of their inspiration. Then "deep calleth unto deep." Then we listen to psalms whose haunting truth and beauty linger so timelessly on the air of the ages that we feel sure the authors were thinking God's thoughts after him. We hear prophets moving so far ahead of their contemporaries that we can explain their words not as the echoes of the crowd but only as the voice of the Eternal. When critics say that what men call the voice of God is only the projection of their own wishful thinking, many words of the prophets rise to refute the charge, for they felt themselves confronted by a God who was not always comfortable. Wishful thinking may call for a merciful God to

---

[3] Isaiah 6:1.

[4] Deuteronomy 33:27.

die *with* but many a prophet as well as the Christ heard the call of a God to die *for*.

If the followers of Christ were to get the wholeness of view given by the Bible in its long panoramic sweep, there would not be so many defections from the church to little ill-informed splinter groups and cults, and there would not be so much defeatism in the wake of disasters and suffering. Recall the scene on the Emmaus road when two adherents of Jesus were leaving Jerusalem in despair after the crucifixion of their leader. A mysterious Presence moved up beside them and asked the cause of their sorrow. When they told him of the cross in Jerusalem, he said, "O foolish men, and slow of heart to believe all that the prophets have spoken! . . . And beginning with Moses and all the prophets, he interpreted to them in all the scriptures the things concerning himself."[5]

If we would love God and Christ with all our minds, we need the wholeness of view given by the Book of Books.

What Is the Fear of the Lord?

"But I do not wish my children to read all the Bible. The Old Testament has so many passages which picture God as a Being to be feared. I want my family to love God, not to fear him." So wrote a sincere and serious mother.

How can the fear of God be reconciled with the love of God? "The fear of the Lord is the beginning of wisdom" is an assertion made both by the psalmist[1] and by the Wisdom Writer.[2] This statement undoubtedly seems out of tune with the mood of our time. Best-selling books offering freedom from our besetting fears pour from the press. With our private worries and our world tensions, why add to the somberness of life by adding the fear of the Lord?

At a League of Nations meeting some twenty-five years ago one of the delegates declared, "We have every fear here except the fear of God." Perhaps the fear of the Lord, if properly understood, might still prove "the beginning of wisdom" in dispelling some fears of our disordered and distempered world.

---

[5] Luke 24:25, 27.
[1] Psalms 111:10.
[2] Proverbs 1:7.

We soon learn in childhood that there are danger spots in life. The child in the nursery discovers that there are things which are hurtful and to be avoided. A friend of mine was telling of watching his two little sons at play in their living room. The younger was quite mischievous, and frequently as he reached for some forbidden object his mother would say, "Ah, ah, don't touch." After this had happened several times the older boy, about nine, said to his younger brother, "Bill, don't you know this is an ah-ah world?" Yes, it is a world with things to be avoided.

Moreover, as the child grows up, he discovers that even if he gets by the danger signals set up by his parents, as well as the danger signals set up by policemen and road signs, there is still a red light of warning which flashes in the chambers of his conscience. Sooner or later intelligent men learn that there is a moral law. And this awareness of a higher justice, overarching the justice of man, is one phase of the fear of the Lord.

And if nothing will restrain a person from wrongdoing except the fear of punishment, then it is salutary and necessary to "put the fear of the Lord into him," meaning thereby to impress him with the inevitable judgments of God.

But decent people do not live in those low moods where they must be kept straight by fear of punishment. They learn that the justice of God is more than a set of warnings. What a dismal time one would have if on a motor tour he looked only for the red lights at the crossings. When a tourist looks at the lofty peak of the Matterhorn, he does not spend his time thinking how fearful it would be to fall off that height. He stands in awe of the mountain's grandeur. The Creator of the heavens and the earth is too great to be thought of as a policeman. When we contemplate the work of God's hands, we rise from cringing fear of his punishments to stand in awe before the majesty of his domain. When I visit London and pass the somber buildings of Scotland Yard, I do not tremble with fear lest some detective come out and seize me, but I am filled with awe at the reach and efficiency of that organization whose fingers comb the gangplanks of steamers from Liverpool to Singapore.

Similarly, when we think of God, unless we are of the lower type of sinners who are ever in fear of punishment, we contemplate his jurisdiction as a majestic system undergirding the universe. The Judaeo-Christian faith holds that God is not only the Supreme Being but the Holy One, the Sovereign and Eternal Good. The "wrath of God," therefore, is not his hatred or anger but the reaction of holiness to anything unholy. And on the Christian's part the "fear of the Lord" is not a feeling of paralyzing fright but one of exalting awe.

Then as we live more deeply into this world we discover that divine justice pervading life is designed for our protection and improvement. God is not primarily a Judge, concerned to preserve his laws. He is a Father, primarily concerned to save his children. "God was in Christ reconciling the world to himself."[3]

And when we contemplate this love of God, our feeling rises from fear to awe to something more, namely reverence. The bad boy is afraid of his father because he fears what his father may do to hurt him. But the understanding adult is afraid of what he may do to hurt his father. He reveres his father. He avoids anything which might cast a shadow on his father's name or heart. Such feeling is akin to the fear of the Lord on its highest level.

What, then, is the fear of the Lord? It depends on what level we are living. Down on the low level of a bad son the fear of the Lord is the fear of his punishments. On the higher level of dutiful sonship the fear of the Lord is reverence for his power and protection and love. And this, says the proverb, "is the beginning of knowledge."

Where Is the Beginning of Wisdom?

When Alfred North Whitehead delivered the presidential address before the Mathematical Association of England in 1916, he chose for his theme, "The Aims of Education." That message has been circulated until it has come to be recognized by educators as a classic. As Whitehead came to the close of his essay, he said: "We can be content with no less than the old summary of educational ideal which has been current at any time from the dawn of our civilization. The essence of education is that it be religious." Then he adds, "Pray, what is religious education? A religious education is an education which inculcates duty and reverence."[1]

---

[3] 2 Corinthians 5:19.

[1] A. N. Whitehead, *The Aims of Education* (New York, 1949), p. 26.

How far does the most formative philosopher of the twentieth century parallel the pronouncement of the Old Testament psalmist, "The fear of the Lord is the beginning of wisdom,"[2] and the writer of the Book of Wisdom: "The first thing in knowledge is reverence for the eternal"?[3]

The essential relationship between religion and education was pretty generally recognized in the American educational system until recent years. The cherished doctrine of the separation of church and state did not deter public schools from opening their sessions with devotional exercises. The ministers of churches were frequent visitors and speakers in the public schools. But now the scene has largely changed. In some states it is not possible to offer any public prayer in public school assemblies. Millions of American youths go through our state educational systems with the impression that religion is either not sufficiently important to be included with the secular subjects of the curriculum or is too fraught with prejudice and superstition to be treated by free minds in free schools.

Our leading educators are alert to the need of inculcating moral and spiritual values, but they feel frustrated by the prohibition of religious teaching in our public schools. Our church spokesmen bemoan what they call the godlessness of our public schools, but they do not reach sufficient agreement to correct the situation.[4] Granted that religious doctrines cannot be included in public school curricula, certainly agreement could be found on the basic principles which would develop duty and reverence.

"Duty," says Whitehead, "arises from our potential control over the course of events. Where attainable knowledge could have changed the issue, ignorance has the guilt of vice."[5] Education is not the mere mental accumulation of ideas but "the acquisition of the art of the utilisation of knowledge." To be sure, one may develop an encyclopedic mind sufficient to answer $64,000 questions on a television show. And that is a value not to be denied! But a person

---

[2] Psalms 111:10.

[3] Proverbs 1:7 (Moffatt trans.).

[4] The situation described here obtains in New York. It varies in other states.

[5] Op. cit., p. 26.

may possess such a memory and yet be quite ineffectual in using his knowledge for the handling of his own life and the welfare of others.

Without a sense of responsibility for his knowledge, a person cannot be a Christian or even a decent citizen. To say that a man is utterly irresponsible is about the worst condemnation we can give. It means that no one can count on him.

But a sense of duty or a sense of responsibility requires an object. It is a duty to someone, a responsibility for something. One object, of course, can be one's own self. I can say, "I owe it to myself to do this or to refrain from that." Self-respect gives some rootage for a sense of duty. But while the ideal of a gentleman is to be inculcated, it is hardly sturdy enough to resist the turbulence of some stormy temptations, nor is it sufficiently social to make an effective member of society.

An adequate sense of duty needs roots which reach out to others, certainly to those nearest to us in our home circle. Some years ago the head of a family addressed a parent-teachers meeting at the Lincoln School in New York City. He said he could see nothing in the modern school curriculum which took the place of his father's early training. He went on to say that it could hardly be supposed that his father as a boy got up at five o'clock in the morning to milk the cows and to keep the woodpile stocked because of his inordinate fondness for those tasks. Rather were they the necessary functions of home life, the daily performance of which fell to his lot, as did other jobs to the other children. This daily rendering of service vital to the well-being of the family developed in the lad the power to make himself do the duty that presented itself wholly apart from how he felt about it, a power that was surely the foundation for the self-mastery which was one of the outstanding characteristics of his life. The boy who did those chores was John D. Rockefeller, and the man who delivered the speech about him was John D. Rockefeller, Jr.

One cause of the current juvenile delinquency is that our city homes lack those family chores of former times. At the earliest possible moment the child in the home needs to learn that he has certain duties and responsibilities to the family.

When the young grow up and enter school or college, they should be made to feel responsible for the institution just as the institution is responsible for them. The growth of personality during student days is effected quite as much by the responsibilities shared as by the courses taken. Recently a dean of a great medical school was discussing the proposed shortening of the liberal arts college training for premedical students in order to permit doctors to begin practice at an earlier age. And the dean very cogently pointed out how the character of students is matured by the responsibilities which come to them as upperclassmen.

Upon leaving school the youth takes a job, usually under someone else at first. Here is another sphere of mutual responsibility. Only as employees feel sincerely obligated to promote the output of their employers, and only as employers feel it their duty to further the welfare of their employees can the industrial scene be healthy. When industry is looked upon as a battlefield between management and labor, we may be able to keep it functioning sufficiently well to produce material goods, but we are missing the main function of work, which is to develop persons rather than products. Work makes character and personality, but only in a climate of mutual responsibility.

When employment is secured and a home is established, the sense of responsibility should extend itself to the community. Family love does not flourish at its best unless it is rooted in community responsibilities. Parents and children should relate themselves responsibly to the institutions and movements of the neighborhood. Loyalty to locality is one of the healthiest signs of good citizenship. This factor is being progressively endangered by the mass living of metropolitan areas. As the group grows, the sense of individual responsibility tends to shrink. That is why the civic life of large cities so often falls below the level of smaller towns. The more we live in large cities, work in large factories, vote in large party machines, the more our minds are victimized by mass thinking and our sense of personal responsibility is weakened.

A few years ago in Calcutta I saw a crowd of fifty thousand people milling around some communist speakers. That crowd was made up of the landless, propertyless, and in large part jobless people of Calcutta—very fertile soil for the communist seed. But when a person builds himself into a community, feeling that he belongs to, and is responsible for, the homes, the schools, the institutions of the place, he becomes quite immune to the communist germ. The spirit of community is one of our best defenses against communism.

Beyond the community, the roots of responsibility run out into the nation. A worthy citizen not only feels it his duty to obey the laws of his government but he also feels responsible for the quality of the laws to be obeyed. It is not enough to keep the law. We must help to keep up the law. And this duty increases with the degree of education. It is appalling to consider how many "smart" persons use their knowledge to find ways of getting around the laws of the land. The greatest peril in our mounting crime statistics is due not to the ignorant but to the educated. Crime has become "big business" in America because of the brains enlisted in its nefarious projects.

The Soviet Union at first vitiated the teaching of science by subordinating it to political propaganda. The scientist was tested by his "regularity" in terms of communist principles. The evil of such a situation eventually became apparent to the communists. The scientist should be free to pursue truth, unfettered by political pressures. The pursuit of truth must take place within the frame of life's wholeness. The scientists who develop hydrogen bombs, sputniks, and guided missiles can hardly clear their consciences by saying that they have no responsibility for the results of their work and the uses to which their products are put.

Education to inculcate duty cannot be limited by national boundaries. The roots of responsibility run out to the ends of the earth and we can no more isolate our consciences from world issues than we can fence off our oyster beds from the tides of the ocean.

On the campus of a big state university the head of the department of religion declared recently that students were not as much interested in large social questions now as in his undergraduate days some twenty years ago. How to "get the most out of life," how to secure a job soon enough to set up a home, how to overcome fears and inferiority complexes, how to find contentment and social acceptance—such, he said, are the issues which get the quickest and widest response among students. How far we can generalize on this professor's statement I do not presume to say. But we shall be in a perilous state if the campus, like the general reading public, prefers self-centered books on peace of mind to the neglect of social problems.

Dark is the future if the graduates of our high schools and colleges do not feel deeply responsible for the reduction of armaments, the improvement of relations between races, the bettering of living conditions among backward peoples, and the other issues on which the world's future hangs.

And then in the midst of all these circles of responsibility stands the church. Sometimes we hear persons say, "I cannot join the church because I cannot take on any more responsibilities just now." Is the church just an added obligation, one more thing to support? So some think. But how wrong! The church stands in our midst to remind us that all the other circles of obligation—our homes, our work, our communities, our nation, our world—revolve around one central and sovereign responsibility, namely, our responsibility to God himself.

John Galsworthy in his drama, *Loyalties*, told of an English army officer who stole from a wealthy Jew who was being entertained at the same house party. He took the money to purchase, on the eve of his marriage, the silence of an Italian girl with whom he had been too intimate. Then the entangling alliances began. The Jew, bitter over being blackballed at a London club, brought suit against the army captain who had stolen from him. The army crowd, motivated by class and racial loyalties, stood by the captain. The Italian girl's father, in devotion to his family, tried to hush the matter up. The captain's wife, in loyalty to her family, stood by her husband. The attorneys refused to take the case out of loyalty to the standards of their profession. Thus the roots of loyalty became so snarled that, as one onlooker acidly said, "Criss-cross, we cut each other's throats with the best of motives."

But were those the best of motives? Loyalty is indeed a high motive, but its adequacy depends on the quality of its object and the frame of wholeness in which it operates. Family loyalty, class loyalty, community loyalty, national and racial loyalties crisscross to cause immeasurable tension and strife. The hope of bringing them into harmony is through a sovereign loyalty. Here, then, is one reason for adding reverence to duty, as Whitehead did in his definition of the essential aims of education. If we are to co-ordinate our responsibilities, "the first thing in knowledge is reverence for the eternal." In our loyalties and loves, the matter of priority has to be settled as it was settled by the Deuteronomic code and reemphasized by Jesus: "You shall love the Lord your God with all your heart, and with all your soul, and with all your mind, and with all your strength. This is the first and great commandment."

How Recover Reverence?

Reverence is to be linked with duty not only in order to co-ordinate our loyalties and responsibilities but also in order to enforce them. Reverence is the profound feeling of awe blended with love in the presence of something regarded as sacred. Our spirits become reverent in those experiences which make us feel that the eternal is touching the moment and the divine is drawing near to the human.

A traveler enters Westminster Abbey. As he walks through the dim aisles he finds himself surrounded by the tombs of England's heroes. The dignity and greatness of man grip his imagination. From the shadowy vaulted arches he feels the centuries looking down upon him. A sense of something greater than man begins to cast its spell over his spirit. Things invisible and eternal engulf the things that are seen and temporal. The dead seem linked with the living. The visitor's voice sinks to a whisper. His spirit is hushed with awe and filled with gratitude. That is the mood of reverence.

The person who lacks reverence lacks high incentive and a dependable sense of duty. Of little force are oaths of loyalty to a nation taken by those who do not believe in God. Of little value are vows taken at the marriage altar by contracting parties who do not feel sanctity when they "plight their troth" in "accordance with God's holy ordinance." The life on whose landscape there are no "sacred" spots is as unresisting to the gusts of temptation as is grassless soil to the dust storm.

Reverence cannot be commanded by sudden fiat. It must be cultivated. John Ruskin suggested some areas of cultivation. He said, "Reverence is due to what is pure and bright in your own youth." Rare is the individual who cannot look back to some luminous moments when God seemed real and some things seemed sacred. Recall the experience of Jacob. When he fled from his father after cheating Esau, the young Jacob had a dream as he slept in the wilderness. His vision was of a ladder reaching up into heaven and of the Lord saying: "I am the Lord, the God of Abraham your father and the God of Isaac. . . . Behold I am with you and will keep you wherever you go." When Jacob awoke he said: "Surely the Lord is in this place; and I did not know it."[1] He called the name of that place Bethel. Years later, as Jacob was returning stained with sin to his father's country to face Esau again, the message which he heard from the Lord was: "Arise, go up to Bethel, and dwell there; and make there an altar to the God who appeared to you when you fled from your brother Esau."[2]

The cultivation of reverence requires going back to our Bethels, a return of our minds to those experiences in our youth when God seemed near.

Ruskin suggests secondly that reverence is due "to what is true and tried in the age of others." A healthy respect for age is a refining influence in the rearing of youth. And in our time we are departmentalizing life too much along age lines. The late John Buchan, governor general of Canada, was wont to tell how he was helped by his association with his elders when he was a young lawyer. Both in our work and in our worship we have become too age-conscious and age-separated. In our churches our children are cared for in youth departments, and in our families there is little sharing of religious experience between the generations to enrich the knowledge and ripen the judgments of the young and also to quicken the insights of their elders.

A third suggestion of Ruskin is that reverence is due to "what is great among the dead." Our hurrying, materially minded generation is more interested in getting ahead than in remembering the past. In the colonial settlement the churchyard with its tombstones helped to keep the dead in remembrance. But in our modern cities the dead are buried in cemeteries outside the circles of active living or hidden

---

[1] Genesis 28:13, 15, 16.
[2] Genesis 35:1.

away in the ashes of the urn. Out of sight, all too soon out of mind. If, as Edmund Burke said, society is a compact between the living, the dead, and the great unborn, then our social health requires a more vital remembrance of the departed. The increasing momentum of change makes more imperative the steadying influence of tradition. We need regularly to be reminded of what T. S. Eliot calls "the backing of the dead."

As the Director of America's Hall of Fame, under the custodianship of New York University, I was asked to pass judgment on a list of the "immortals" of the first half of the twentieth century. The list of fifty as compiled by a popular magazine contained the name of Al Capone. I said that I could not approve any list as famous while the notorious gangster was included. The reporter replied, "Why not? Al Capone will be talked about for centuries. The Borgias were not good but they are still talked about. That is fame." No, notoriety is not fame. As Henry Van Dyke said, notoriety is to fame as a loud noise is to noble music. Reverence for the great among the dead helps to keep us from being deafened and misled by the noisy among the living.

And Ruskin climaxes his suggestions for the cultivation of reverence by reminding us that it is due to what is "marvelous in the powers that cannot die." When we see men as immortal souls, we have the foundation of reverence for personality. When we feel that our treatment of a child may be shaping his eternal welfare, we handle him with care. Thus again reverence for the eternal is the first thing in the knowledge of human relations.

Sholem Asch, in his *Three Cities*, written a few years after the Soviet Revolution of 1917, told of a young convert to communism who kept asking his comrades whether they believed in the immortality of the soul. They ridiculed his question by telling him that such a question was irrelevant to the great revolution they were leading, that it is only this world that counts, and to ask about the next serves to blur the vision and blunt the impact of reform. But the young convert found their arguments left him feeling that the communist atheism was like the action of a woman who had emptied a feather bed and was trying to pick the feathers up one by one. The weakness of communist education, which will become more apparent with the passing years, is that it leaves out the first thing in knowledge, which is reverence for the eternal.

When Does Believing Become Seeing?

The Galilean fishermen who set out to follow Jesus did not begin with cool speculation and academic discussion. They heard Jesus talk and were astounded at the force and authority of his words. They saw him healing the sick and were amazed at his power. When he came through their villages and said, "Follow me," they felt the lure of his personality and left their nets to go with him.

Should we criticize those fishermen as foolish, saying that they were carried off their feet by emotion? Should they have waited for further proof before they started to follow Jesus? Their neighbors no doubt said yes, but, looking back from our perspective, we answer no! Jesus Christ did not try to sweep people off their feet by senti- mental emotions, but he did want them to have enough emotion to get on their feet and start a course of action. As we have said in Chapter 2, let us not discount the service rendered by genuine emo- tion. A cold engine never starts a train. Some warmth of feeling is needed to get us going toward anything worth while.

When we set out to follow Christ before we understand fully what discipleship means, we are not foolish or sentimental or unscientific. We are taking the attitude required in all true learning. The child in the home must obey his parents at some points before he under- stands the reasons. As we become sophisticated, we think it realistic to say, "Seeing is believing." But in some areas it is also true that "believing is seeing." Augustine put the issue, "Seek not to under- stand that you may believe, but believe in order to understand." A husband must believe in his wife before he understands her. Yes, even if he never comes to understand her!

Belief must outrun reason, though it should not outrage reason. Christ, I repeat, would not sweep us off our feet sentimentally but he would put us on our feet so that we can get going mentally.

Then, having started in Christ's school, the disciple is led toward understanding. The Master Teacher reached the place where he said to his pupils: "No longer do I call you servants, for the servant does not know what his master is doing; but I have called you friends, for all that I have heard from my Father I have made known to you."[1] He had kept them with him while he spoke to the crowds, and then he took them off by themselves to explain some of the secrets of his public utterances and parables. He had them along when he healed and when he went off with them to pray in quiet. Progressively he initiated them into the secrets of his motives and methods. On the last night of his earthly life he told them that he had many things yet to say unto them but these would be revealed to them later when he was away in person and the Holy Spirit had come upon them.[2] When Jesus was crucified his disciples did not know all about him, but they knew what he was about. They had risen from the status of uninformed servants to that of friends who shared in his thoughts.

How Understand God's Rewards?

And when the disciples of Christ rose to the status of friends, they entered into a new understanding of the rewards of loving service. With apparent paradox, Jesus, the preacher of disinterested love, talked frequently of rewards. For instance, "If you lend to those from whom you hope to receive, what credit is that to you? Even sinners lend to sinners, to receive as much again. But love your enemies and do good, and lend expecting nothing in return; and your reward will be great and you will be sons of the Most High."[1]

It was not easy for the disciples to fathom Jesus' principle of reward. When the rich young man was told to go and sell his possessions if he would join Christ's company, Peter spoke up and asked, "Lo, we have left everything and followed you. What then shall we have?"[2] Jesus replied that they would be repaid a hundredfold and would inherit eternal life. Then he told the parable of the vineyard workers, some of whom bargained in the morning with the vineyard owner. Others came along at the third hour and the sixth hour and the ninth hour, and went to work without any stipulation of pay.

---

[1] John 15:15.
[2] John 16:12–13.
[1] Luke 6:34–35.
[2] Matthew 19:27.

When settlement came at the close of the day, they all received the same wage.

The point of the parable is that God's rewards are sure but they are not to be bargained for. This world is not a factory wherein the wage agreements are signed in advance. This is Our Father's world and we are the children of God, not bargaining but trusting. The followers of Christ are his friends, putting in life for love. Jesus did not endorse the neat little dogmatic explanation of prosperity as the mark of divine approval or the currently popular interpretation of prayer as insurance against adversity.

It is the incalculability of reward which is the mark of God's love for us and the prerequisite of our love for him. If the payments for virtue could all be calculated, life would no more develop one's faith than operating an adding machine develops one's mathematical skill. There could be no true love in a cut-and-dried world where rewards are guaranteed. Mother love would not be worthy of the name if it measured its care of children by calculating what they can do in return when they grow up. Mothers give extra care to little crippled children who will not be able to repay and to little sick boys and girls who will never grow up.

In our relation with Our Heavenly Father we are to work in love and faith, not looking for the return. Thereby we develop a deeper love and a larger faith.

When we rise in our thinking to "worship God in spirit and truth," we see how faithful is his law of spiritual harvest: ". . . whatever a man sows, that he will also reap."[3] The farmer sowing his wheat may not always get a good crop, but the patience and resourcefulness which he puts into his work bring forth a harvest of greater patience and resourcefulness and he becomes a better farmer. The artist applying his interpretive powers to the canvas may not always receive an adequate financial reward for his effort, but he does acquire a greater power of portrayal. The person who pours out his love on another may not always be compensated by the return of the other's love, but he does develop a deepened appreciation of love, a greater capacity for love, and makes himself more lovable.

---

[3] Galatians 6:7.

The most beautiful description of love ever penned was written by one who had been ostracized from his home, persecuted, imprisoned, stoned. Thus he learned the resiliency and invincibility of love: "Love bears all things, believes all things, hopes all things, endures all things. Love never ends."[4]

What about the Mystery of Evil?

When we bid men to love God, we meet on every hand those who question whether God is lovable. Sometimes the doubt arises from bitter personal experience. Shortly after the war a grief-stricken mother cited this situation. She said her neighbor was a frivolous woman who neglected her son and allowed him to grow up too weak to be accepted by the draft board. On the other hand, she had taken good care of her boy and developed him into fine sturdy manhood. Her son was drafted into the army and lost his life. She queried, "Where is the love of a God who lets a careless parent keep her son and takes the beloved boy of a devoted mother?"

Others deny the goodness of God from a broader and more philosophical viewpoint. They point out that nature is "red in tooth and claw," that creation is a curious mixture of stars and snakes, of beauty and poisons, of trade winds that aid commerce and tornadoes that tear up towns and strew the ground with lifeless bodies. How can we declare that God is lovable when he allows innocent babies to be born blind and bombs to drop on inoffensive populations, where the good often die young and licentious roués live to a ripe old age?

We cannot stop to expound here some of the familiar answers given to these plaintive queries. Since the time of Job wise men have realized that in the vastness of creation it is not possible to trace clear lines of cause and effect in suffering. Our finite minds must trust the infinite beyond the bounds of our seeing.

We know, too, that we should distinguish between what God allows and what he intends. God as a Father, in order to rear his children, must give them freedom of choice. If they choose courses of conduct which bring on disasters and wars, the fault is with the

---

[4] 1 Corinthians 13:7–8.

creatures, not with the Father. God does not intend that men shall kill themselves on highways and battlefields, but restrained by his own fatherhood he must allow them to make their own decisions. In his omniscience God foresees the suffering of his children, but he does not foreordain it.

Yet these explanations still leave us bewildered by the mystery of evils which befall us through nature rather than through human nature, such as hurricanes, tidal waves, floods, and their like. These disasters, which in legal terminology are called "acts of God," may be explained by natural law but it is hard to reconcile them with divine love.

Perhaps one purpose of these seemingly bad things is to help life to be good. How could there be goodness if there were no badness to overcome? How could there be courage if there were no dangers? How could there be faith and hope if there were no doubt and despair to be faced? How could there be love if there were no misunderstandings to be reconciled? Without things which hinder and oppose us, life would lose the factors which help us. When we are flying we like a tail wind to give us speed, but in order to start or stop a plane we have to have a head wind. Unless there were friction we could not start or stop a train. A certain amount of life's so-called evils serve a purpose similar to that of head winds and friction. They help us to handle life. They keep nature in balance.

Is Goodness Not a Greater Mystery?

When we confront the mysteries of evil, we should recognize that they are exceeded by the mysteries of goodness. Why wind should become twisted into a tornado and hit one Texas town while it skips another is indeed beyond our understanding. But the orderliness of nature which enables the pilot to steer through blinding storms by radar is a still more profound mystery. We can explain the hatred of men as love become bitter, but we can hardly explain love as sweetened bitterness. After witnessing the futility of war and its mounting destructiveness, it seems madness that men should still think they could insure their welfare by killing. But warmakers are still less of a mystery than the martyrs of love. Why should a man lay down his life for his friends, and why should a Christ go to the cross to save his enemies? Great as is the mystery of evil, greater is "the mystery of godliness."

St. Paul did not stop with awe at the mystery of God's creation. Between Job and Paul, Jesus had revealed a God whose love awakens reverence rather than mere trust. Job was facing in the right direction when he continued to believe though he could not see. But Jesus Christ came as "the way, the truth and the life" by which men could advance from the stoical fortitude of Job to a confidence in the saving grace of God. Saul of Tarsus experienced this saving grace and after enduring a testing as severe as Job's declared triumphantly, "We know that in everything God works for good with those who love him, who are called according to his purpose."[1]

Paul is no sentimental optimist trying to persuade his readers that all bad happenings are blessings in disguise. Paul is not saying what a minister once said glibly to the parents of a deformed and demented child—that the sending of such a child was God's way of blessing them by testing their faith. What Paul asserts is that God co-operates in all things "for good with those who love him and are called according to his purpose."

Note the words again, "God works *for* good." Things which are good *for* us do not always seem good *to* us. We do not always know at the time what is good for us. A father does things to his children which they may think bad because they do not understand his good purpose. So Our Heavenly Father may do things which our finite minds feel to be dire hardships, and yet through them he is working for our true welfare.

And then Paul adds the qualifying clause, "who are called according to his purpose." What is God's primary purpose for our good? Physical health? No, not always. Worldly success? No. Our good, according to God's purpose, is to grow up into the likeness of his Son, Jesus Christ. Paul is not saying that God will turn all our physical sufferings into physical blessings and all our defeats into social and financial victories. But God does co-operate in all things with those who love him to use whatever happens as steps to more Christlikeness. And that is our highest good.

---

[1] Romans 8:28.

The Epistle to the Hebrews joins Paul in throwing light on how to transform the mystery of evil into the mystery of good. After the familiar eleventh chapter on faith, in which the writer depicts the heroes in Israel's Hall of Fame, he opens the next chapter by bidding his readers not to "regard lightly the discipline of the Lord nor lose courage when you are punished by him; for the Lord disciplines him whom he loves and chastises every son whom he receives."[2]

It would be presumptuous for our finite minds to say what proportion of our sufferings are due to the discipline of divine love. We do look back on our childhood and understand now how some of the parental punishments which at the time we thought undeserved were designed for our good. We also remember the occasions when we were sent up to some dark room or denied some desired pleasure and mother would say, "This hurts me more than it does you." Such words seemed unreal to us at the time. But now that we have become parents—and especially if we are grandparents!—can we see a little girl go weeping to her room or hear a little boy sobbing himself to sleep because he is being punished, and not suffer more than the child?

When we look back along the course of our lives, cannot we all point to some experiences which seemed cruel disappointments at the time but later proved to be the kindly discipline of Our Heavenly Father's chastening? How grateful I am that God did not give me some of the things for which I longed! In things we have suffered and in things we have been spared, thoughtful retrospect reveals the discipline of divine love.

And if we keep rooted in a spirit of love for God, these chastening experiences do work toward our maturing.

Leigh Hunt, speaking of Napoleon after he escaped from the island of Elba and made his stand at Waterloo, wrote, "No great principle stood by him." When Napoleon faced the troops sent to take him prisoner, he exerted all his old personal magnetism and won the soldiers over to be his followers. He led them to Waterloo for the final stand. But the glamor of his name and the brilliance of his generalship were not enough. As was said, "No great principle stood

---

[2] Hebrews 12:5–6.

by him." And his last days as a prisoner at St. Helena were filled with remorse and mental anguish.

I think by contrast of a man who was almost meteorically successful until he was about forty years of age. Possessed of a most attractive personality and business acumen, he rose by a path of unbroken success. Then through no fault of his own came reverses which swept away his savings. But his spirit did not break because he had strong religious principles which did stand by him. In those difficult days he went down pretty far, but he discovered that "underneath are the everlasting arms." His nature became mellowed, his judgments more charitable, his sympathies wider. And he became one of the most genial, understanding, effective Christian gentlemen I have ever known.

When a person is rooted in the love of God and sustained by trust in the purpose of God, adversity serves to help him mature. The cut flower withers in the heat of the sun, but the flower in the ground is made by that selfsame heat to grow and blossom.

Consider the qualities which make a full, rich, beautiful life: patience, which gives us poise and perseverance; forbearance, which keeps us from flying off the handle and withholds us from pressing our advantage against weaker persons; fortitude, which enables us to bear our own burdens without whining; sympathy, which enters into the sufferings of others; humility, which prompts us to confess our own weakness and sin; generosity, which leads us to forgive others and grant the benefit of the doubt and the boon of service—all these qualities are grown in soil which has been plowed by some deep experiences and harrowed by some penetrating afflictions.

St. Paul declared that three times he besought the Lord to remove his physical ailment. The answer which Paul received was not the removal of his "thorn in the flesh" but this promise: "My grace is sufficient for you, for my power is made perfect in weakness."[3] Relying on that assurance, the Apostle wrote triumphantly: "For the sake of Christ, then, I am content with weaknesses, insults, hardships, persecutions and calamities; for when I am weak, then I am strong."

In an earlier book I have written that I regard the mixture of the

---

[3] 2 Corinthians 12:9–10.

sad and the joyous experiences of life as analogous to a ship. There are parts of a ship so heavy that by themselves they would sink—the engine, the propeller, and other features. But built together in a ship, they float. Recently my faith has been reinforced by this added thought: the parts of a ship which are heavier than water are necessary to make a ship sail. We cannot use a boat unless there is weight enough to give it draught. We even put in ballast to make it serviceable. Likewise in life, without these heavy experiences which sometimes threaten to sink us, our lives would lack the ballast to keep them going.

Yet despite all analogies and scriptural quotations, this discussion cannot answer all the queries of a bewildered or suffering reader. All our science and philosophy form only an island of knowledge surrounded by an ocean of mystery. The larger the island grows, the longer the shoreline where the known meets the unknown. Our knowledge still halts where Paul's did and says with him: "Great indeed, we confess, is the mystery of our religion."[4]

But our lack of knowledge need not mean a loss of faith. We can remember what Paul also said: "Now we see in a mirror dimly, but then face to face. Now I know in part; then I shall understand fully, even as I have been fully understood. So faith, hope, love abide, these three; but the greatest of these is love."[5]

---

[4] 1 Timothy 3:16.
[5] 1 Corinthians 13:12–13.

5 WITH ALL YOUR STRENGTH

When Strength Comes

FROM SELF-STIMULATION

FROM A POWER BEYOND THE SELF

FROM A SENSE OF DIVINE VOCATION

FROM AWARENESS OF GOD AT WORK WITHIN

FROM THE FEELING OF BELONGING TO GOD

FROM THE DIVINE COMMUNITY

When Strength Comes

To love God with all our strength is to give our utmost to the highest. How far short we come from the fulfillment of this commandment was apparent to Jesus when he declared, "The sons of this world are wiser in their own generation than the sons of light."[1] In the parable which Jesus told to illustrate this truth, the dishonest steward displayed an energy and ingenuity in promoting his own welfare far surpassing that which the professed followers of Christ devote to advancing the kingdom of God.

Not only do we fail to use our full strength in the love and service of God, but we do not even know the sources and limits of our own potential. Strength is a very deceitful thing. In the matter of physical strength, a thoughtful person realizes that he cannot always trust his feelings as accurate. It frequently happens that the bodily organ we think the strongest proves the weakest. Also in emergencies we demonstrate undreamed-of power.

In our spiritual natures it is even easier to be deceived. How often it happens that a person is weakest at the point where he thinks himself strongest. Our good traits of character are in us somewhat as the grain is in the wood. The grain gives beauty but it is along the grain that the wood can be split. Similarly it is along the grain of his virtues that a man's character is most easily cracked. We are in more danger from the traits of which we are proud than from the traits of which we are ashamed.

FROM SELF-STIMULATION Before we go very far in life we have to

―――――――
[1] Luke 16:8.

learn the sources from which we draw our strength. We may possess strong constitutions, stout hearts, alert minds, disciplined wills. These factors of strength should not be minimized in these days of cafeteria education and psychiatric manipulation.

A certain amount of self-reliance is essential to effective living. Emerson wrote that "self-trust is the first secret of success." Worthy self-reliance is a firm but modest dependence on one's own abilities and efforts instead of a weak and unmanly leaning on outside assistance. If a person does not possess this trait, he will be the football of his fellows and the sport of circumstance. Self-reliance is a staff for the pilgrim and a tool for the worker.

And we surprise ourselves by what we can do through sheer force of will. The old copybook maxim, "Where there's a will, there's a way," had a valid stimulus. To be sure, its recent recrudescence in some contemporary modes of preaching, which promise that we can do anything if we only believe we can, has led many to mistake bootstrap self-help for the lift of the "everlasting arms." Nevertheless, will power and self-reliance need to be stressed, not as substitutes for divine help, but as steps to it.

And although psychiatry has produced its charlatans and developed too many dependents, we can justifiably count on the power of the unconscious. We have discovered that the hidden dynamo of the unconscious can be made to work for us. We have found that our minds are most susceptible to heartening and energizing thoughts at certain times, as for example in the early morning. It has been said that the first twenty minutes determine the day. We now realize that the unconscious can work wonders for us even while we sleep, for we have found that sleep not only can knit up "the ravelled sleeve of care" but can often untie the knotty problem which baffled our waking hours.

But we are not mere self-starting units. After we have come through an experience in which we displayed unexpected, even inexplicable, strength, we sometimes say, "I did not know it was in me." Well, was it in us? In January 1954 a two-hundred-foot schooner carrying a group of scientists from Columbia University was battling mountainous seas north of Bermuda. Something went wrong with the steering gear. Suddenly four men were swept overboard.

One of them was Professor Maurice Ewing, distinguished oceanographer. Death seemed inevitable but after a harrowing struggle he was rescued. The next day he wrote a letter to his five children. He said that out in the waves, faced seemingly with certain death, he felt he could hear his children calling to be saved from drowning and he must keep swimming to save them.

Summing up his experience, he wrote: "As a scientist I naturally think first of physical things. . . . But I know, too, that something more than the merely physical was involved in my being able to survive. We must remember about love. The love that your children, your mother and I have for each other gave me strength to keep afloat long after I was exhausted. Your love—little Maggie calling to me—was stronger than those terrible waves. God's love brought the ship to us before the steering gear broke again. We may not be able to understand fully the power of love, but it is very real, and is one of the most important things in the world."[2]

FROM A POWER BEYOND THE SELF   Shall we say that the increased power felt by Professor Ewing in the submerging waves was merely the self-stimulation which love gave to his heart and glands? Or did it come from a "Power not ourselves that makes for righteousness"? In the realm of physical science men talk about "vibration frequencies" and "radiations." Hence some say that if we believe God is a spirit and that the spirit in every human breast is embedded in the divine Spirit, then it is permissible to think that a fervent prayer may initiate currents of energy which gather strength and direction as they flow through Infinite Understanding and Love.

Analogies between physical and spiritual vibrations seem to me a bit confusing and unnecessary. Our language is so colored by material concepts that it has not the terms in which to describe the spiritual realm. It is hard to improve on the simple non-technical testimony of St. Paul regarding "him who by the power at work within us is able to do far more abundantly than all that we ask or think."[3]

Yet, in appraising and applying the "power at work within," let

[2] *Reader's Digest*, September 1954.
[3] Ephesians 3:20.

us not discount the necessity of our own effort. The current advice to "relax, relax" may often be good for the nerves but it must not weaken our nerve. The cult of easy religion cannot countermand the first half of the apostolic order, *"Work out your own salvation with fear and trembling; for God is at work in you, both to will and to work for his good pleasure."*[4]

Consider the case of Jeremiah. As a young prophet he had started out with high hopes. But he was cruelly disappointed in the results of his work. The king had sought his counsel and then had refused to follow it. The overseer of the temple had him put in the stocks for public ridicule. The people of Jerusalem had acclaimed him and then turned against him. Jeremiah was ready to quit. Then he tells us that he heard the voice of the Lord saying unto him, "If you have raced with men on foot, and they have wearied you, how will you compete with horses?"[5]

That word was a call to the latent manhood within him. It awakened Jeremiah to the pettiness of his plaintive mood. It was a sort of Old Testament version of the modern expression, "Cheer up, the worst is yet to come."

Hard to measure is the extent to which we can be stirred by stern summonses and hard situations. But while such a stimulus serves to quicken a flagging pace, it is not adequate to keep us going long. It is necessary to feed the mind as well as flog the will. A good coach does not merely urge his team "to play up and play the game." He builds them up in body and morale. Similarly Christ in training his immortal eleven did not merely urge them to follow him. He built up their morale with hope, saying, "Fear not, little flock, for it is your Father's good pleasure to give you the kingdom."[6] He teamed himself with them so closely that they felt the magnetism of his touch and the exhilaration of his comradeship. "Take my yoke upon you, and learn from me. . . . For my yoke is easy, and my burden is light."[7] Religious faith has a power-giving force far surpassing moral appeal. Morality says, "Here is the rule of righteousness, follow it."

---

[4] Philippians 2:12–13.
[5] Jeremiah 12:5.
[6] Luke 12:32.
[7] Matthew 11:29–30.

Christian faith says, "Here is the spirit of goodness, receive it." To receive the grace and power of God involves the will, but the will serves to arouse a strength already resident in us. "I remind you to rekindle the gift of God that is within you through the laying on of my hands; for God did not give us a spirit of timidity but a spirit of power and love and self-control."[8]

FROM A SENSE OF DIVINE VOCATION   In stirring up God's gift of power within us, the motive is important. Professor Ewing struggling in the Atlantic waves, as described above, found strength given him because he felt that he must save his children. The measure of strength received from God depends on the degree of selflessness in man's motive. The great souls of history have made it their ideal to let God work *through* them rather than *for* them. If we wish to feel the full power of prayer, we must seek it not for our own use but in order to be used of God. When we assemble in church on Sunday, we call it a service of worship. Service for whom? To be sure, it is in part to serve our own needs, to lift our burdens, to calm and clear our minds. But churches are not meant to be the spiritual counterparts of the "service stations" which line our highways to supply us with gas and oil for driving. Church services are primarily designed to give people power and direction in serving the purposes and programs of God.

Saying this, we do not wish to imply that the programs of God to be served are limited to those promoted under church auspices. All work, personal or social, secular or ecclesiastical, can be conceived and empowered as a divine vocation.

Arnold Toynbee asserts that the concept of "work" as distinguished from idleness or play arose only about eight thousand years ago. Before that time man, like other animals, had to exert himself to keep alive, but he simply took what he found in human nature. Then some eighty centuries ago man discovered that he could make the earth produce by cultivation. This origination of agriculture came about through man's efforts to appease the gods of fertility. Thus work, distinguished first in agriculture, stemmed in a sense from religious worship.

---

[8] 2 Timothy 1:6–7.

Toynbee continues his thesis by declaring that the concept of work was later deconsecrated into secular economics. The Graeco-Roman conquests created situations wherein the manual labor was done by the enslaved many for the benefit of the idle aristocratic few. When the Christian religion arose, it restored a certain dignity to manual work because its Founder was a carpenter and its first devotees were drawn from the humbler walks of life.

Then, some five centuries after Christ, St. Benedict initiated a most significant advance in the concept of work by incorporating manual labor as an integral part of spiritual discipline. The Benedictine brothers were to spend part of the day in physical toil and part in religious devotion. By thus reconsecrating man's work, Benedict imparted to it the potent driving force of religious enthusiasm.

Toynbee's point in treating the history of work is that it becomes satisfying personally and far more productive materially when it is infused with spiritual purpose. "Man at work can be happy and spiritually healthy only if he feels that he is working in God's world and for God's glory through doing what is God's work."[9]

If we are to love God with all our strength, we must erase the traditional distinctions between spiritual and secular work. We make a grievous error in thinking of spiritual work as those activities done within the walls of churches or under the auspices of religious organizations. Not what we do but why we do it determines the spirituality of our work. Doctors, engineers, farmers, factory workers may be quite as spiritual as ordained ministers. It has been said that to some clergymen their duties are just a job, while to a truly Christian plumber his work is a vocation. One is tempted to add that the latter is a better paid vocation than that of many a cleric! Bishop Richard Emmerich arrestingly asserts that ninety-five per cent of a church's work is done outside its walls by its members in their daily labors.

A sense of divine vocation is essential to releasing our full strength in our work. This does not require that we think of our particular job as one which God has chosen for us, or that it is necessarily the best position which we could have filled. But we do need to

---

[9] *Man at Work in God's World*, edited by George E. De Mille (New York, 1956), p. 15.

feel that we are workers together with God in doing something worth while. Yes, and we may prate about the dignity of labor and the sense of divine vocation, but if we are to vitalize these concepts, we must change some of our social estimates. As long as manual laborers and mental workers are separated by residential sections and social caste, there is a hollow sound to our assertions that we are all "workers together with God."

FROM AWARENESS OF GOD AT WORK WITHIN   The Christian is strengthened not only by his awareness of working for God but also by his feeling that God is working in him, "for God is at work in you, both to will and to work for his good pleasure."[1] A recognized scientist figures that a farmer's toil is five per cent of the energy expended in producing a crop of wheat. The other ninety-five per cent is the universe taking advantage of the chance which the farmer gives it. The love of God for us is the fertilizing and fructifying force at work in us to bring forth the fruit of the spirit—love, joy, peace, and their like.

To this truth John Wesley came by a hard road. In 1725, at the age of twenty-two, Wesley set himself to a most rigid self-discipline in the hope of getting right with God. It was thirteen years later that he experienced the glow of heart which transformed his painful and unsatisfying struggle into the creative force which made him the formative religious figure of eighteenth-century England. And historians of the Methodist movement which Wesley founded assert that his doctrine of "Christian perfection" delivered the aspiring soul from "the insupportable burden of seeking to achieve holiness by personal toil and opened the door to achievement by God's gift of perfect love through faith in Christ."[2]

How to blend activity with receptivity in the proper proportion is a secret of spiritual strength. When we feel God is at work in us, he does not repeal the first half of the law: "Work out your own salvation with fear and trembling." But he transforms craven "fear and trembling" into creative carefulness as of one who handles trust

---

[1] Philippians 2:13.
[2] William E. Sangster, *The Path to Perfection* (New York, 1943), p. 102.

funds with more care than his own possessions. "You are not your own; you were bought with a price."[3]

Alcoholics Anonymous stipulates as its first step in reclamation the admission by the victim of the drink habit that he is unable to handle his problem and needs higher help. It is not merely bidding him to "cast his burden on the Lord"; it is calling him to co-operate with God, conscious of his worth in God's sight and of his responsibility as a partner with God in conserving precious values.

Aware of God at work within us, we are kept from thinking too highly of ourselves and also too meanly of ourselves. We are humbled out of that "cockeyed cocksureness," to use Galsworthy's term, which distorts vision and leads to the collapse of cleverness. It is a curious fact that we overestimate our strength when we think about possible temptations and underestimate our strength when we look ahead at possible troubles. If someone warns us to stay away from a seductive situation, we say, "Oh, I would never yield to that temptation." Yet we do so often yield. On the other hand, we contemplate some possible calamity and say, "I could never stand that." Yet if the trouble overtakes us, we do come through.

God at work in us gives us perspective as well as insight. We little men move about our daily rounds somewhat as a spider crawls up the outside wall of the skyscraper apartment house in which I am writing. It comes to a jutting stone, and what a barrier the stone appears. It reaches an overhanging eave and what a topsy-turvy thing the structure seems. What conception can that spider have of the architecture of this skyscraper? So we move about amid the immensities of God. We are prone to judge the nature of things by the little haunts and grooves we know. When our outlook is thus limited, we have no perspective which can prepare us for untoward circumstances. We need to be lifted out of our littleness and with the psalmist raise our eyes unto the hills. And to realize with him that our strength cometh from the Lord, who made heaven and earth.[4]

When we glimpse the greatness of God at work within us and see things in longer perspective, we see that barriers which seemed in-

[3] 1 Corinthians 6:19, 20.
[4] Cf. Psalms 121.

surmountable can be overcome, that hills of difficulty which appeared so impossibly steep at a distance do seem to level out a bit when we start climbing. And when this larger look gives us assurance that God is at work in us for a purpose, then comes a surge of strength. Purposeless work proves unendurable.

> *Tomorrow, and tomorrow, and tomorrow,*
> *Creeps in this petty pace from day to day,*
> *To the last syllable of recorded time:*
> *And all our yesterdays have lighted fools*
> *The way to dusty death. Out, out, brief candle!*
> *Life's but a walking shadow, a poor player*
> *That struts and frets his hour upon the stage*
> *And then is heard no more: it is a tale*
> *Told by an idiot, full of sound and fury,*
> *Signifying nothing.*

In contrast to the dreariness of such meaningless living, those who "wait for the Lord shall renew their strength, they shall mount up with wings like eagles, they shall run and not be weary, they shall walk and not faint."[5] The surge of the divine Spirit gives those soaring moments in which we leave our low-vaulted past and rise to the grand vistas of eternal purpose and enduring ends.

Professor Bliss Perry, lately of Harvard, wrote that, when a student at Williams College, he once complained to his father, a professor there, about the time wasted in chapel service. His father replied that if you are turning a grindstone every moment is precious, but if you are doing a man's work the inspired moments are precious. There are occasions when we must take time off to take eternity in. Through God-illumined gaze we behold the glory of the common place and the divine in the daily round. As Stefan Zweig said of Dickens, God "unveils the poetry that was ambushed in the prosaic," and gives to "simple and unpretentious people a glory all their own."

Some years ago my son, a sixteen-year-old lad in a boys' school, wrote a class poem which he entitled, *Travelers of the Plains*. Two lines from that poem are carved above his grave:

---

[5] Isaiah 40:31.

> *Living's tiny land is mostly plains*
> *And ecstasy's swift singing mountains*
> *few and far between.*

Life's land is mostly plains. The dead levelness of it becomes monotonous and the luminous hopes of youth "fade into the light of common day." For this reason middle age is the most dangerous age spiritually. The goals which beckoned at twenty-five seem as far away at forty-five. It is then that men are tempted to lower their spiritual hopes and sometimes to loosen their moral harness.

"They who wait for the Lord shall renew their strength . . . they shall run and not be weary." Feeling God at work within them, men get a "second wind" of the spirit. Their mood is more than stoic fortitude. It becomes radiant hope. "We rejoice in our sufferings, knowing that suffering produces endurance, and endurance produces character, and character produces hope, and hope does not disappoint us, because God's love has been poured into our hearts through the Holy Spirit which has been given to us."[6]

The long perspective which God gives stretches beyond the limits of our own strength, even of our life span. In the familiar eleventh chapter of Hebrews on faith, the author calls the roll of Israel's Hall of Fame: Abraham, Jacob, Moses, and the other heroes of the great tradition. He pictures them as pursuing divine promises which they never fully attained. "These all died in faith, not having received what was promised, but having seen it and greeted it from afar."[7] How cruel of God, do we say? But here is the paradox: when we are aspiring to reach something beyond our grasp, we do better the things within our grasp. Consider King David. He cherished four great desires. He wanted to win his people's wars, to unite his people into a nation, to establish his nation's capital at Jerusalem, and to crown that capital with a temple to his nation's God. David never built the temple. But his overarching dream helped him to do better the things within his range.

> *Ah, but a man's reach should exceed his grasp,*
> *Or what's a heaven for?*

---

[6] Romans 5:3–5.
[7] Hebrews 11:13.

FROM THE FEELING OF BELONGING TO GOD   To love God with all our strength involves still another source of power. It is found in the feeling of belonging to God. There is a vital difference between longing for God and belonging to God. The contrast was revealed in the words of Paul on the deck of the doomed ship on which he was bound for Rome as a prisoner. The other passengers were undoubtedly calling on their gods to save them. But Paul felt a different relationship to his God. After much abstinence and prayer he stood forth in the midst of the despairing crowd and cried: "I now bid you take heart, for there will be no loss of life among you, but only of the ship. For this very night there stood by me an angel of the God to whom I belong and whom I worship, and he said, 'Do not be afraid, Paul; you must stand before Caesar; and lo, God has granted you all those who sail with you.' "[8]

This vision of Paul's was a mystical insight beyond our power to explain. But it demonstrated that Paul was living a two-dimensional life, that he was in communication with plans to which his own were secondary, and that he felt guided by a wisdom greater than his own. All this gave Paul a strength derived from a sense of destiny. He had completely surrendered his life to God and he believed that God was using him for a purpose and that God would not let his life go until this purpose was accomplished.

When men assert that they are destined to accomplish certain ends, listeners are likely to be skeptical, for destiny, like liberty, has had many crimes committed in its name. The Napoleons and the Hitlers have left a sorry trail. But we must distinguish between a feeling of destiny born of prayer and one born of power. Paul's vision came after "much abstinence and prayer"; Napoleon's star rose with the expansion of his egotistical power. Paul's sense of destiny developed through self-surrender and suffering; the dictator's boast of destiny is bred from ambition and success.

When a person, after prayer and sacrifice, is convinced that he is destined to fulfill a purpose of the Lord to whom he belongs, he has a security and strength "able to do far more abundantly than all that we ask or think."[9] When Andrew Melville was threatened by the

---

[8] Acts 27:22–24.
[9] Ephesians 3:20.

Earl of Morton with hanging if he did not cease his free speaking, Melville answered in words dear to Scotsmen: "Tush, sir, threaten your courtiers after that manner. It is the same to me whether I rot in the air or in the ground. It will not be in your power to hang or exile the truth." Intelligent men seek the truth to make them free from error, clever men may use the truth for their purposes, but consecrated men feel themselves used by truth, and that gives them a power for surpassing mere self-expression or self-expansion.

Moreover, the Christian's strength derives not only from the purpose which he is fulfilling but also from his personal relationship with the God to whom he belongs. God is a Designer who will not let his plans be frustrated. He is also a Father whose love will not allow his consecrated children to be taken from him. "Who shall separate us from the love of Christ? Shall tribulation, or distress, or persecution, or famine, or nakedness, or peril, or sword? . . . No, in all these things we are more than conquerors through him who loved us."[1]

Others since Paul's time have felt the same personal security in being held by God's guiding hand. Dr. Edmund Wilson, distinguished physician and naturalist, was one of the party of five that reached the South Pole with Scott in 1912. On the return journey one man collapsed and died when more than halfway back. Another went out and gallantly accepted death to spare his friends the burden of caring for him. Wilson and two others trudged on. The loss of his comrades and his own impending death did not shake his confidence in God. In his diary he wrote: "So I live, knowing that I am in God's hands, to be used to bring others to Him, if He wills by a long life full of work, or to die to-morrow if He so wills, having done nothing worth mentioning. . . . We must do what we can and leave the rest to Him. . . . My trust is in God, so that it matters not what I do or where I go."[2]

FROM THE DIVINE COMMUNITY The strength which comes from the sense of belonging to God is not fulfilled if it is treated as a private privilege. An only child in a home loses something which

---

[1] Romans 8:35, 37.
[2] George Seaver, *The Faith of Edmund Wilson* (London, 1948), p. 44.

comes from sharing parents with brothers and sisters. A Christian must feel himself a member of God's family.

Professor A. Victor Murray of Cambridge asserts that in a full-orbed Christian faith there are five elements: something to know, something to feel, something to choose, something to do and something to belong to.[3] Belonging to the community of God is an essential part of the Christian gospel. The Christian must seek within the Christian community opportunity for further light and further service.

It is a mistake to think of the Christian church as a factor added by his followers to the gospel which Christ preached. The church is integral to the teaching of Christ. We speak today of the "young churches" being organized in India, Africa, the Philippines, and elsewhere. America itself is a land of comparatively young churches. We are in danger of limiting our thought about the age and nature of the church by the dates and methods of organization. We must ever be reminding ourselves that the church of Christ is the Body of Christ and that his "Body" was not born after his crucifixion at Pentecost. The church of Christ came in the gospel of Christ. And it was "a new covenant in his blood"—a renewal and revision of the old covenant by which Israel felt bound.

The individual needs community for his own spiritual health and strength. There is danger, of course, that individuality may be ironed out by organization pressure and mass living. We need periods of aloneness to preserve our personalities. But personality cannot be developed in a vacuum. Spiritual growth requires a proper blending of solitude and group activity.

Sometimes we get the impression that we could be good if others were not around to tempt us. But temptations are often succumbed to more readily when we are alone than when we are in company. In the Genesis story of Eden the account records that Eve was alone when the serpent beguiled her. Milton in *Paradise Lost* picked up this fact to imply that she was most susceptible to temptation when she was away from her partner. And Dr. George Hunt in his arresting book, *Rediscovering the Church*, carries the point further by

---

[3] A. Victor Murray, *Education into Religion* (New York, 1953), p. 14.

asserting that when Eve was away from Adam she was less than her full self. He stresses the idea that isolationism opens the door to temptation. All of us know the lures which are harder to resist when we are removed from familiar social sanctions and are feeling the pangs of loneliness.

And if this be true of physical temptations, it is even more true of those temptations which tug at the mind. It was when Our Lord was alone in the wilderness that the tempting suggestion came to him. And at his Last Supper Jesus said to his disciples, "You are those who have continued with me in my trials ["temptations" in King James Version]."[4] It would seem that Jesus, sinless and perfect though he was, chose his disciples not only to train them but also to strengthen himself with their comradeship.

A sense of community gives the individual strength not only by the encouragement imparted to him but by his enrichment through the demands made upon him. When some request for help taxes our strength, we discover our resources. When others bring us their doubts to be cleared up, we explore the strength of our own beliefs. When a friend looks at us with great, large, round eyes of pain or sorrow and asks us to pray for him, we test and extend the power of our prayers.

"Giving is the highest expression of potency. In the very act of giving, I experience my strength, my wealth, my power. This experience of heightened vitality and potency fills me with joy. I experience myself as overflowing, spending, alive, hence as joyous. Giving is more joyous than receiving, not because it is a deprivation but because in the act of giving lies the expression of my aliveness."[5]

Erich Fromm, illustrating the above statement from the spheres of psychology and sex, is giving support to the prayer attributed to St. Francis of Assisi: "O Divine Master, grant that I may not so much seek to be consoled as to console; to be understood as to understand; to be loved as to love; for it is in giving that we receive; it is in pardoning that we are pardoned; and it is in dying that we are born to eternal life." The paradox of strength is that we get by giving.

The Christ, who demonstrated the secret of community strength

---

[4] Luke 22:28.
[5] Erich Fromm, op. cit., p. 23.

in the company of the twelve, was aware that only as a group could his disciples carry on his work. As separate individuals they could not have stood up against the pagan pressures of their time. Even Paul, whose power seemed so Christ-centered that he could say, "I can do all things in him [Christ] who strengthens me,"[6] needed community support: "I long to see you, that I may impart to you some spiritual gift to strengthen you, that is, that we may be mutually encouraged by each other's faith, both yours and mine."[7]

If the individual requires fellowship in community to sustain his own strength, it is even more apparent that he needs group membership to multiply it. History furnishes many examples of what strong personalities can achieve. We can cite the work of towering figures in almost every age who seemed to turn the tide of events. Closer inspection, however, reveals that the individuals who appeared to shape events were in reality riding the crest of a tidal wave of co-operating forces. For instance, we can say that Martin Luther led the Protestant Reformation, but we could not say that he created it. Luther with all his personal force and courage would have been crushed had not the German princes been ready to revolt against overweening ecclesiastical power.

Or turn from religion to business. We look back to the titans of industry—the Carnegies, the Fords, the Rockefellers—and we are impressed by the power of single individuals. But even their impact derived from the resources which they channeled. And in their places today stand corporations, run by many men with influence and importance all down the line. Progressively business is counting on Organization Man.

One of the most subtle and baffling problems of modern living is to preserve personal initiative and responsibility in the midst of increasing organization. As the group grows the individual tends to shrink. In a city of a million the per capita civic interest is less than in a town of ten thousand. The long production lines of a large factory dwarf the creative impulse and pride of work which inspired the artisans of an earlier day.

---

6 Philippians 4:13.
7 Romans 1:11–12.

In counteracting this dwarfing pressure of numbers the ingenuity of civic and economic leaders will involve many factors, but among these the contribution of the church grows ever more important. As the spirit of community is being weakened by mass living, it becomes more imperative to strengthen the sense of community through religion. The church must remind the person who feels lost in the crowd that he is still under the eye of God. The individual who thinks himself helpless in the midst of a giant corporation must be made aware that he has a corporateness in the church. Through the Body of Christ of which he is a member, the Christian can take hold of levers long enough to reach the ends of the earth and lift the burdens of backward peoples. In the councils of the church pooled wisdom can be applied to the most complex social problems, and through the corporate voice of the church counsel can be given which governments cannot with impunity ignore. Only through belonging to the community of God can we show our love for him with all our strength.

We are strengthened by the thought that we are carrying on a great tradition. At the 1948 Olympic Games in London a dramatic incident occurred in front of my section of the stadium. A relay race was on. The French team had started well. But as the baton was being passed to the third runner he dropped it. The accident, of course, put the team out of the running. The runner threw himself to the ground, flung his hands to his head in a gesture of despair, and openly wept. His emotional outburst continued as he was led from the area.

To take defeat so tearfully might seem a bit unsportsmanlike. But one should remember how many persons were involved in that runner's failure. There were his watching compatriots, whose hopes were dashed. There were the two teammates who had run before him and whose work was ruined by his blunder. And then there was the runner who was to come after but who never got the chance to run because of the accident.

The whole spectacle made me realize how much life is like a relay race. In the race of life, no one starts from scratch, each for himself. Others have run the course before us and we start from the point where their lives touch ours. Our parents come down the track, for a while we run along beside them until they are able to pass the baton of their work and character on to us. Then we carry on while our parents slow down and eventually drop out of the race. Ultimately we come around to the day when we transfer our interests and unfulfilled hopes to our children. Thus generation is linked to generation.

This resemblance of life to a relay race is borne out by the writer of the Epistle to the Hebrews. His beloved eleventh chapter quoted above ends thus: ". . . all these, though well attested by their faith, did not receive what was promised, since God had foreseen something better for us, that apart from us they should not be made perfect."[8] Thus Scripture suggests how each generation is called of God to perfect the faith of its forerunners and through this linkage of love to fulfill its own strength.

Furthermore every normal person wants his work to go on after his death. We rejoice to have families who will carry on. We desire to give ourselves to causes which will keep going. Here is a climactic reason which turns thoughtful men to the church.

The Christian church is the oldest and vastest organization actively at work in our midst. It has survived the Caesars and belted the globe. Despite the mediocre morality of its members, the frequent mismanagement of its material interests, the deplorable divisiveness of its sects and denominations, the church of Christ has survived and spread until his followers now number over six hundred million. The earthly defects of the Christian church attest the divinity of its origin and support, for only God could have kept the church going and growing. The divine life which flows through the Body of Christ must be in us if we are to love the Lord Our God with all our strength.

---

[8] Hebrews 11:39–40.

PART TWO

6 LOVE'S DOUBLE LIFE

Love That Comes Naturally
Love That Does Not Come Naturally
Love That Does Not Come at All

The first commandment, great and inclusive as it is, cannot stand alone. Matthew and Mark record Jesus as adding immediately and voluntarily a second. "And a second is like it, You shall love your neighbor as yourself. On these two commandments depend all the law and the prophets."[1] Yes, and each depends on the other.

Our love for God requires love for our neighbor in order to prove itself. It means little or nothing to ourselves or to others if we say that we love God but do not show it in love to our neighbors. In *John Brown's Body*, Stephen Vincent Benét pictures the captain of a slave ship who was faithful in his prayers but saw nothing wrong about his traffic in human bodies.

Tradition has it that Sir John Bowring, as British governor of Hong Kong, promoted the opium trade with China. Yet Sir John wrote the tenderly moving hymn,

> *In the cross of Christ I glory,*
> *Towering o'er the wrecks of time;*
> *All the light of sacred story*
> *Gathers round its head sublime.*

Because men can thus think that they love God regardless of their attitude toward others, the First Epistle of John flares forth with these flaming words: "If any one says, 'I love God,' and hates his brother, he is a liar; for he who does not love his brother whom he has seen, cannot love God whom he has not seen."[2]

Jesus in his description of the Last Judgment makes it clear that

---

[1] Matthew 22:39–40.
[2] 1 John 4:20.

the redeemed are those who had shown their love for God by their ministering to the hungry, the sick, the poor, even to the least.[3] At the Last Supper, Our Lord gave the supremely identifying mark of discipleship: "By this all men will know that you are my disciples, if you have love for one another."[4]

That the love of neighbor is required to attest our love of God is a theme stressed by the contemporary pulpit, perhaps to the point of triteness. But let us go on to say something not so familiar. It is that by loving one another we learn to love God.

How would a lad learn to love God as a Father if he had never known parental love? A theological student, working in New York's East Harlem among Puerto Ricans under slum conditions, reports that it is futile to talk to his young people about the fatherhood of God. The only concept of a father which many of his hearers have is of the male adult who hangs around the flat and perhaps helps them occasionally to escape the police coils. In the loose marital morals prevalent there, children are not sure of their parentage. Only through the experience of a father's love can we appreciate Christ's portrayal of God.

Or suppose a person had never made any sacrifice for others, had never put himself out to help others, how would you explain to him the principle of the cross of Christ? How could such a man understand the love which led Christ to serve those who never paid him, to heal those who never thanked him, and at last to pray for those who were putting him to death? The love and sacrifice shown to those around us are the steps by which we climb to comprehend the "breadth and length and height and depth, and to know the love of Christ which surpasses knowledge."[5]

Johan Bojer, Scandinavian novelist, wrote of an engineer whose little daughter was killed by a neighbor's dog. The cruel loss drove the father almost insane. At first it shattered his faith. Shortly afterward the region was stricken with famine conditions. The engineer took some of his meager supply of seed corn and planted it in the field of the neighbor whose dog had slain his little girl. Let the be-

---

[3] Matthew 25:31–46.
[4] John 13:35.
[5] Ephesians 3:18–19.

reaved father describe the mood and motivation of his conduct: "Now it was that I began to realize how every great sorrow leads us farther and farther out on the promontory of existence. I had come to the outermost port now—there was no more.

"I understood how blind fate can strip and plunder us of all, and yet something will remain in us at the last that nothing in heaven or earth can vanquish. Our bodies are doomed to die and our spirits to be extinguished, yet still we bear within us the spark, the germ of an eternity of harmony and light for both the world and for God.

"More and more it came home to me that it is man himself that must create the divine in heaven and on earth—that that is his triumph over the dead omnipotence of the universe. Therefore, I went out and sowed the corn in my enemy's field that God might exist.

"So marvelous art thou, O spirit of man! So god-like in thy very nature! Thou dost reap death, and in return thou sowest the dream of everlasting life. In revenge for thine evil fate, thou dost fill the universe with an all-loving God."[6]

Marvelous, indeed, is the spirit of man that can return good for evil and replace hate with love. By such conduct we do make God come alive in our hearts. Thus love of neighbor gives reality to love of God. But in all this man is not the originator. He is a worker together with God. He is fulfilling the apostolic injunction to "work out your own salvation with fear and trembling; for God is at work in you, both to will and to work for his good pleasure."[7]

Love That Comes Naturally

The amazing love potential manifested by the bereaved father may seem to stem from the spirit of man, but "The spirit of man is the lamp of the Lord."[1] Consider the analogy of the lamp in that pre-electric time. The flame was fed by the inflammable ingredients of the candle. Similarly in man there are manifestations of love which appear to be fed spontaneously by the elements resident in his hu-

---

[6] Johan Bojer, *The Great Hunger* (London and New York, 1918), p. 321.

[7] Philippians 2:12–13.

[1] Proverbs 20:27.

man nature. The infant demonstrates a form of self-love, an instinctive desire to satisfy his own needs. He wants what he wants when he wants it. Then comes love of parents, an outgoing affection for mother and father. A little later appears the love of friends, usually those of the child's own sex. After a while something in the youth feeds that first pure flame of adolescent love which shows in the sparkling eyes of teen-age boys and girls. Later comes the love of mate, which forms the family and enriches the natures of both husband and wife. Normally this is followed by parental love, which is the most selfless, persisting even when it is not reciprocated.

In all these forms of love man seems to "do what comes naturally." However, the apparent naturalness of such love should not cause us to dismiss the divine element. It is God who has put the instinct of sex into our bodies and the hunger for affection into our hearts. He lighted the fire of love, and man's expanding knowledge has not explained the mystery of birth by which God passes the torch of life and love from generation to generation, nor has man's wisdom dispelled the wonder of love in its simplest forms.

Love That Does Not Come Naturally

But there are manifestations of love in which men do more than "what comes naturally." Left to themselves, men do not "fall in love" with neighbors on the other side of the equator, or even on the other side of the railroad tracks. It does not "come naturally" to help neighbors whose dogs have killed our little daughters or to forgive enemies who have slaughtered our sons in battle. Our natural affections do not go out spontaneously to the unlovely and the disagreeable.

Toyohiko Kagawa, the Japanese Christian leader, whose experience before and during and after the Second World War gives him warrant to speak with authority on the subject, distinguished three levels of love. The first is physical love, which holds persons together in families. Kagawa would also classify as physical love the bonds which bind individuals to their nation or labor union or any other group which benefits them materially.

Above this level is a plane which he calls psychic love. Every true marriage rises above physical attraction into an affinity of minds and interests. Psychic love also includes our association in friendships, in professional and social groups, and in all those relationships which rest on community of mental tastes.

Above the psychic Kagawa posits a still higher level of love which rests on conscience. If one is walking along the road with an enemy on his right hand and a sinner on his left, and if he can walk with them without accusing them or if he can halt his progress to help them, then he has risen to the plane of conscientious love. Such was the love which Jesus manifested and to which he summoned his followers, bidding them do good to those who hated and persecuted them. Such love is too high for those who do just "what comes naturally."

As truly as our love for God requires love for neighbor to give it reality, so our love for neighbor requires divine love to give it stimulus and scope—yes, and safeguards also.

Love That Does Not Come at All

Despite the fact that Jesus made love for God and love for neighbor the central imperatives of Christian conduct and declared that on these two commandments "depend all the law and the prophets," it is astounding that Christ's professed followers treat these two so much less strictly than they observe the "Thou shalt nots" of the Decalogue. The person who breaks the commandments "Thou shalt not steal" and "Thou shalt not kill" is taken into custody by the state. If he violates the commandment against adultery, the laws of the church take cognizance. But if he transgresses the law "You shall love your neighbor as yourself," what happens? Does the state or the church step in to condemn the man who is lacking in love? No.

There have been and are situations in which to be lacking in love for other human beings is a way to rise in the opinion of church and state. In the early 1940s any American who openly proclaimed his love of the Germans under Hitler would have been socially ostracized if not physically interned. In the 1950s American citizens who professed friendship for the Soviets were under suspicion as subversive. And in some communities the most vociferous and venomous haters of non-white neighbors win applause, even political votes.

Why is it that we treat the commandment to love so much more loosely than the Ten Commandments? Perhaps the difference in attitude is somewhat analogous to our treatment of traffic lights. "Thou shalt not," like a red light, means "stop," and we stop whether we are driving a truck or a Cadillac. "Thou shalt love," on the other hand, like the green light, means "go." But we go at such different speeds.

A St. Francis of Assisi dashes ahead with a love which goes out to lepers and outcasts, and we feel that is too impossibly noble for us and we let him pass. Then there are those who love people of other races enough to fraternize with them, and we say that they belong to the "left" and so we pull over to the right and let them go by. And Jesus of Nazareth sets forth with a love that goes so far as to pray for his crucifiers and we feel that to be perfectionism completely beyond us. Hence most of us just hug the "right" side of the road and love along at any pace we like. In short, we allow the commandment "You shall love your neighbor" to lapse into a standardless sentimentalism.

What can we do to correct this situation and give brotherly love sufficient specific content to make it Christian?

7 AS YOU LOVE YOURSELF

How Do You Love Yourself?
How Reliable Is the Golden Rule?
Is a Sense of Honor Sufficient?

How Do You Love Yourself?

Eight times in the Bible appears the command, "You shall love your neighbor as yourself." Its last appearance is in the Epistle of James, and on that occasion the author calls it the "royal law."[1] James may have felt justified in using this high appellation because his Lord had made this law so central in his gospel. The test of brotherly love runs through the teachings of Jesus as the red thread runs through the ropes of the British navy to show that they belong to the Crown. Also this command might be called the "royal law" because it exercises a certain rule over the others, as we have seen in the case of the first commandment.

This law gives the royal measure by which to test our love for God and also for our neighbor. We are to love our neighbor as we love ourselves. But how are we to love ourselves?

John Calvin called self-love a pest. And certainly love of self in the form of pride is the first of the traditional seven deadly sins. In so far as self-love means selfishness, self-centeredness, egoism, it is the very negation of godliness.

Freud equated love of self with "narcissism," and in that form it is ridiculous as well as repulsive. The person who admires himself and is ever preening himself on his good points is a prig and a bore. The fellow who, as we say, "is stuck on himself" is usually stuck with himself. Nobody else wants him.

Certainly such forms of self-love furnish no yardstick by which to measure love for one's neighbor. But to love oneself does not mean to like oneself. A healthy normal person often dislikes himself for

---

[1] James 2:8.

what he is doing, often criticizes himself, sometimes punishes himself. Yet through all his self-criticism and self-chastening he loves himself in the sense that he is seeking his own highest good. He has good will (*agape*) toward himself.

To love yourself in the scriptural sense means that you long to keep yourself worthy of your own self-respect. It means that you desire what the old Edinburgh weaver prayed for each Sunday: "O Lord, give me a high opinion of myself." And to look at yourself in the light of God's love does heighten your opinion of your own value. You see the price God put on your life in that he sent his Son to save you. Muretus, a Christian scholar of the sixteenth century, fell ill while on a journey. Some doctors were called in to treat him. They did not know him and, as he looked rather unprepossessing, they said, "Let's try an experiment on this fellow, for he looks of no importance." From the shadow of the bed came the patient's voice: "Call not any man cheap for whom Christ died."

The godly man loves himself in that he seeks to develop his divine potentialities. Jesus did not flatter men by telling them how good they were. He made them aware of the sin rooted in their nature. He caused them to feel how far short they were of their possibilities. Jesus humbled his hearers but he did not humiliate them. He turned them to a purging repentance for their sins but not to a paralyzing remorse. He kept ever before men the high goals God expected them to reach and the power by which they could attain them. It is noteworthy that the Christ who summoned men to be "perfect as your Father in heaven is perfect" was also called the "friend of sinners." However he might humble them by the consciousness of their shortcomings, he gave them back their self-respect.

To love yourself is to regard your mind as an instrument of God, too precious to be prostituted to unworthy ends, to look upon your body as the temple of the Holy Spirit and hence not to be desecrated by debasing behavior, to see yourself as an immortal soul freighted with immeasurable possibilities for the long future.

And this respect for yourself is a yardstick by which to measure your appraisal of your neighbor. As you have regard for the sanctity of your own person, you must have regard for your neighbor's person. As you value your convictions, you are to recognize the value which your neighbor puts on his views. As you prize your freedoms, you must help to safeguard the liberty of others.

How Reliable Is the Golden Rule?

All these phases of neighborly love are commonly summed up in what is called the Golden Rule: "Whatever you wish that men would do to you, do so to them."[1] This rule, so simple in concept and so concise in phrasing, is not so simple in specific application. It requires more imagination than most of us exercise. Too many of us do not make the effort to picture what we would wish done to us if we were in the others' places, with the result that *we* do to them what *we* think is good for them and that often irritates *them*. The Golden Rule practiced without imagination is often sheer irritation.

Yet we need more than imagination to see how we would wish to be treated if we were in another's place. The teacher looks at the pupil who has broken rules. It is not enough to ask herself, "What would I want done to me if I were in this boy's place?" The lad very likely wants to be let off, but is that best for the boy? The teacher must appraise the pupil's desire of the moment in the light of his longer future. To practice the Golden Rule requires more than imagination. The rule itself must be ever tested by divine standards.

A distinguished judge recently sent a letter to the bishop of a certain communion. The bishop had asked the judge to suspend the sentence of a member of his church who had been convicted of a certain crime. In his answer the judge wrote: "The sentencing of prisoners is one of the most painful duties of a judge. It requires prayerful consideration by all of us. It requires that we consider the offense for which the prisoner was convicted and also the effect of the sentence upon other persons similarly tempted. I say this not with the feeling that either the church or the judges should be vindictive, but rather that they should realistically apply those principles for which our religion stands so as to prevent other people similarly tempted from succumbing to temptation."

Consider another situation. A patient is ill with a fatal disease.

---

[1] Matthew 7:12.

Should a friend or a physician tell him the absolute truth about his condition? We realize that a person who is sick cannot stand the shock of bad news as can a person who is well. We know, too, that hope is a great elixir to a patient. Shall we, then, tell him that his illness is fatal? It is a difficult question and a heavy responsibility. A doctor once remarked in my presence, "To tell a patient that his case is hopeless is to assume the role of God." Hence that physician did not presume on God's knowledge. But he did seek the guidance of the Great Physician in trying to find how to blend truth with hope and love in handling his patients.

While the principles of the gospel are simple, their application requires intense study, illumined imagination, and most prayerful sympathy. It requires godliness to keep the Golden Rule from going off the gold standard.

Herein is a point to be watched in those circles which prate about "reverence for personality" as an improved substitute for the moral codes of the Judaeo-Christian tradition. To be sure, personality is not to be sacrificed on the altars of principle. Institutions and laws are made for man and not the reverse. "The sabbath was made for man, not man for the sabbath."[2] But the rightful desires of men are not to be determined by finding the highest common denominator of the crowd's wishes nor are the basic standards of decency determined by taking the lowest common multiple of the crowd's moral scruples. Reverence for personality without reference to certain recognized divine standards would result in moral confusion comparable to the tangle of time which would be caused by consulting individual clocks without reference to the Greenwich standard.

We need to set self-respect and the Golden Rule in the divine frame of reference not only to get their measure but also to give them dynamism. Self-respect, however safeguarded against subjectivism, does not furnish an adequate motive. When the rich young man came to Jesus asking the secret of eternal life, he was told to keep the commandments of the Decalogue. He promptly replied that he had observed these from his youth. Jesus then said: "You lack one thing; go, sell what you have, and give to the poor, and you will

---

[2] Mark 2:27.

have treasure in heaven; and come, follow me."[3] It would appear that Jesus was testing the young man's motive. Was his morality motivated by his regard for himself and his desire for eternal life or by his love for others? How much did he really care for the poor? Jesus would test his love by bidding him sell his goods and give. It is one thing to have sufficient self-respect to keep oneself pure and honest. It is something more to care enough for others to make real sacrifices for them.

As a motive, self-respect is too negative to be creative, too self-centered to be Christlike. When Jesus commanded, "You shall love your neighbor as yourself," he was calling men to keep a love, not to keep a law. When our motive is merely to keep laws, our method is to conform; when our motive is to keep a love, our method is to create. The lover is ever thinking up new ways to please and serve his beloved. The follower of Christ is ever seeking and finding new ways of loving his neighbor.

Is a Sense of Honor Sufficient?

As love of neighbor requires self-respect and something more, so it also involves and yet transcends codes of honor.

Of a certain man it was said that he served with honor and not for honor. The distinction is apparent. The word "honor" may refer to a motive of service or to a mark of recognition for service. In the latter sense, honor may derive, as Thomas Hobbes asserted, from the mere possession of power regardless of the motive or morality involved. To prove his point Hobbes cited the Greek gods. Jupiter was famed for his adulteries, and Mercury was celebrated for his frauds and thefts. Yet they were honored for their power despite their immoralities.

Three centuries have passed since Hobbes proclaimed such an amoral conception of honor. But his ideas are not everywhere outmoded. Eve Curie, in *Journey among Warriors,* tells of interviewing the first batch of German prisoners captured by the Russians. She asked them if they thought their Fuehrer was right when he invaded Poland. They promptly replied, "Yes." Then she inquired if they thought Hitler was right when he invaded France. They quickly

---

[3] Mark 10:21.

answered, "Yes." Next she asked if they thought their leader was right when he attacked Russia. Since they were prisoners of the Russians at the moment, they hesitated and admitted that Hitler had made a mistake there. From that conversation Eve Curie distilled the conclusion that in the Nazi philosophy the only criterion of right and wrong was, "Does it succeed?" If a plan succeeded, it was right. If it failed, it was wrong.

But we of the Judaeo-Christian tradition do not believe that honor rests on power and popularity. We hold that some things are right and honorable even though they seem to fail, and that some things are wrong even though they seem to succeed. We believe that the sense of honor is not merely the echo of the crowd's opinion.

Honor is not an essential of our physical nature. A person does not have to possess it in order to live. And honor is not necessary for material success. It often happens that those without a very high sense of honor emerge from the rough-and-tumble of competition with their purses pretty well filled. Honor has been defined as moral refinement. Charles Heimsath says that honor is to morals what courtesy is to conduct. This comparison, however, does not connote the full strength of honor.

Some fifteen years ago Van Wyck Brooks wrote that he did not think communism would sweep America as it had Russia, for the reason that we are the heirs of the age of chivalry while Russia was never affected by the literature and ideals of that tradition. Having missed the romance and codes of chivalry, the Russian people succumbed to the materialistic principles of Marxism.

Consider the force of honor. Although not one of our instinctive physical drives, it is often stronger than these.

Hunger, for instance, is a basic drive of our bodily nature. Man will do almost anything to satisfy his physical hunger. Almost, but not quite. The histories of battles and besieged garrisons and exploring parties repeat the records of men who will suffer the agony of gnawing hunger rather than break into the allotted rations and poach from the common store. What is it that keeps a person from stealing his comrade's rations? Fear? Not always. It is something more—a sense of honor.

Sexual desire is another instinctive drive, so strong that some psychologists interpret it as conditioning almost all conduct. And, to be sure, it has turned Caesars into silly slaves of passion and torn countless homes from their roots. But men have found a self-mastery able to subdue this tumultuous passion and to preserve the purity of the home. What is it that restrains the sex urge? Fear? Not always, by any means. There is also the sense of honor.

Love of money is another impulse so powerful that it has been called the root of all evil. Many historians would have us believe that the economic motive overshadows all others. Yet think of Spinoza grinding lenses for a living while he pondered his thoughts of life and God. Louis XIV of France offered him a pension and patronage if he would dedicate even one book to His Majesty. But because Spinoza did not approve of Louis he would not prostitute his talent for what he considered an unworthy end, no matter what the reward.

Go one step further. We take for granted the old saying, "Self-preservation is nature's first law." And when a person is cornered into the choice between life and death, is there anything so powerful as the desire to live? Well, there is something which sends firemen into burning buildings to rescue sleeping babies, something which keeps sailors at their posts of duty while passengers are sent away to safety in lifeboats, something which has strewn history with heroic deeds of self-sacrifice. It is that something which we call a sense of honor.

Honor is so basic to life that some call it the bedrock of character. Yet saying all this, we must go on to see that honor has to be safeguarded and strengthened by godliness.

Codes of honor need ever to be made more inclusive in their application. Sometimes they are limited by class boundaries. The medieval knights treated the fair ladies of the nobility with all the honorable considerations of chivalry but they would defile the daughters of the peasantry without compunction of conscience or censure of their class.

Think how codes of honor are often narrowed by racial lines. The white colonizing nations observed different codes according to color lines. Strongly as we condemn the communists for their devilish methods of infiltration in Southeast Asia, we cannot blame communism for all the evils in that region. The colored races of those regions are slow to welcome the help of white nations like ours because of what they have suffered at white hands. The powers that once promoted colonialism are reaping the harvest of race discrimination and false codes of honor, however they may repudiate the former practices.

Also our codes of honor must be made more dynamic as well as more inclusive. Too often we pride ourselves on playing the game as gentlemen but give no thought to improving the game. Some years ago Harold Begbie drew a devastating description of Herbert Asquith, a former Prime Minister of Britain. His characterization may not have been accurate, but Begbie said of the urbane, learned, gentlemanly Asquith that his scholarship had made no difference to scholarship, and his moral earnestness had made no difference to morality. Begbie asked if we could imagine Asquith with a profound and reverent anxiety striving like a giant to make right, reason, and the will of God prevail.

It is one thing to be decent enough to have a distaste for unrighteousness; it is another to be good enough to have a hunger and thirst after righteousness. It is one thing to be sufficiently respectable to obey the law; it is another to be sufficiently godly to improve the law. It is good to be a gentleman who stands by his word; it is better to care enough for truth to find out the facts and make one's word worthy to stand by.

Sometimes in our complex and baffling world we are tempted to think that all that can be expected of us is just to be "decent and let the devil take the hindmost." But suppose all our ancestors had been content just to be decent according to the codes of honor prevailing in their group and time. There would then have been no St. Francis of Assisi going out to leaven the sodden mass of medieval poverty, no John Howard setting forth to cleanse the prisons of Europe, no Lord Shaftesbury sacrificing himself for the poor outcasts of London, no Lincoln reaching out his great roomy arms to lift a race from slavery to selfhood.

Only because some of our forefathers had a godliness more dynamic than mere decency do we have the blessings which we now enjoy. And only as we preserve and practice their creative goodness will there be a better world tomorrow.

8 LOVE IN THE DAILY ROUND

When Love Grows Wild

When Love Is the "Fruit of the Spirit"

> LOVE IS "PATIENT AND KIND"
>
> LOVE IS "NOT JEALOUS OR BOASTFUL"
>
> LOVE IS "NOT ARROGANT OR RUDE"
>
> LOVE "DOES NOT INSIST ON ITS OWN WAY"
>
> LOVE IS "NOT IRRITABLE OR RESENTFUL"
>
> LOVE "DOES NOT REJOICE AT WRONG, BUT
> REJOICES IN THE RIGHT"

When Love Grows Wild

The flowering of love is often beautiful in the wild. The seeds of love seem so embedded in the soil of human nature that they spring up in lovely forms without cultivation. The debutante who has flitted about in carefree butterfly existence before marriage becomes a young mother, and beautiful indeed is the devotion she gives to her child. Parenthood deprives her of her former parties, chains her to a crib, and wakes her in the night with petulant cries. But while a young mother needs training in the care of her child, no normal mother has to be taught to love her child. Mother love comes naturally and is beautiful even in the uncultured wilderness.

With all the current psychiatric search for peace of mind, the artist seeking to illustrate its attainment could find no better subject than the face of a little child nestling against his mother's breast. The infant's attachment to his mother is a beautiful outcropping of love, common to all climes and colors, and it needs no cultivation to produce.

But ponder the words of George Eliot in *Felix Holt:* "The mother's love is at first an absorbing delight, blunting all other sensibilities; it is an expansion of the animal existence; it enlarges the imagined range for self to move in; in after years it can only continue to be joy on the same terms as other long-lived love—that is, by much suppression of self and power of living in the experience of another." Such suppression of self and vicarious power does not come naturally. It requires cultivation of the spirit.

The first budding of romantic love has a freshness of beauty wherever found. So great is its thrill in the wild state that some hold it should not be tamed by social regulation. Marriage, they maintain, is a convention which removes the bloom of spontaneous love.

When Love Is the "Fruit of the Spirit"

Yet the testimony of long experience is that love in the wild state does not keep its fragrance and beauty. Man has an animal nature but he is not meant to run wild. Man is not basically a body possessed of a spirit. He is primarily a spirit equipped with a body. The scriptural sequence is: "God created man in his own image."[1] "God is spirit."[2] And "the fruit of the Spirit is love."[3]

Love, the "fruit of the Spirit," is the product of the divine Spirit at work in the soil of human nature. It is the result of infinite cultivation on God's part. It requires persevering co-operation and cultivation on man's part.

If we would appreciate this cultivation, consider the experiences out of which comes the most beautiful and comprehensive description of love extant. It was composed by a man who by nature was disposed to be rigid in his convictions, narrow in his racial outlook, suspicious of new ideas. Prostrated by the impact of a new doctrine which shook the foundations of his former religious faith, he arose to risk his life in devotion to a movement which caused him to be ostracized by his family and often brought him into controversy with the other leaders of his new-found cause. Imprisoned, persecuted, stoned, he suffered almost "all the ills that flesh is heir to." Yet he came through rejoicing in his sufferings, knowing that "suffering produces endurance, and endurance produces character, and character produces hope." Why? ". . . because God's love has been poured into our hearts through the Holy Spirit which has been given to us."[4]

And this quality of love which the Apostle Paul had cultivated he carried into a querulous company of new Christian converts at Corinth. The church founded there by Paul had split into factions. Some said they belonged to Paul, others adhered to Apollos, an eloquent preacher from Alexandria who had followed Paul in the

---

[1] Genesis 1:27.
[2] John 4:24.
[3] Galatians 5:22.
[4] Romans 5:3–5.

Corinth parish; still others asserted allegiance to Peter, whose pres-
tige in the apostolic church had its appeal. And others, probably in
derision at this divisive spirit, said they were of Christ. Paul sought
to heal the divisions by leading them back to the divine source of
their blessings. "I planted, Apollos watered, but God gave the
growth."[5]

What kind of love was Paul, the gardener of God, trying to grow at
Corinth? That port city was familiar with love in the wild. Corinth
had been the proving ground of Greek culture. To this city came
Paul preaching "Christ crucified, a stumbling-block to Jews and
folly to Gentiles, but to those who are called, both Jews and Greeks,
Christ the power of God and the wisdom of God."[6] And then Paul,
out of his own experience of the love of God in Christ, enters into a
description which with unparalleled beauty brings divinely begotten love into the daily round.[7]

Familiarity breeds ever growing appreciation of the sentences.

LOVE IS "PATIENT AND KIND"   The hot passion of the blood may be
impetuous and impatient but in divinely cultured love patience is
an essential ingredient. What patience is required of a parent to
adjust the pace to little toddling steps that stray aside, to answer
without irritation the repetitious questions of little lips, to patch up
broken toys and mend broken hearts. And what patience it takes to
keep marriage from losing its romance, to adjust diverse tempera-
ments, to harmonize conflicting interests, to wait for moods of stub-
bornness to pass, to be teamed with a life partner who at times does
not seem to be pulling his or her share of the load. Patience to endure
the daily round without lapsing into dullness, patience to live under
the same roof year after year without letting the nearness get on
your nerves, the patience of forbearance which withholds the hasty
word and the patience of forgiveness when the hurtful word has been
blurted out—such patience does not grow wild. It is a "fruit of the
Spirit."

And, says Paul, love is both "patient and kind." Love, to be kind,

---

must have more than a vague general kindheartedness. It must be sufficiently skilled to be kind in specific situations.

Sir Lawrence Jones, in *A Victorian Boyhood,* looks back to his school days and declares that compassion is not learned by suffering but is the fruit of happiness, that to experience social unkindness leads to aggressiveness, and that if he were a headmaster he would be more concerned with the vice of unkindness than with any other moral failing in his school.

Consider what patient kindness it takes to be loving toward those who are older and feebler. Some persons grow old so gracefully that they invite kindness as rich, ripe fruit invites the tasting. But others allow themselves to descend into a self-centered decrepitude. When we look at a man who has fallen into a crotchety and cranky feebleness, we should look at him somewhat as we gaze at the ruins of a noble cathedral and try to imagine him in his prime when his body was "the temple of the Spirit." The patience and kindness of love are developed by a considerateness and cultivation which require godliness to sustain.

LOVE IS "NOT JEALOUS OR BOASTFUL."   Love on the natural level is possessive and exclusive. In our common speech the connotation of love is a game or chase in which the lover pursues his beloved, is jealous of his competitors and proud of his conquest if successful.

Some years ago A. S. M. Hutchinson, the English novelist, described the marriage of two very competent people. The union gave every promise of succeeding. Both were able and financially independent. But before long the wife came to the conclusion that all a man marries for is to have a place where he can keep his books, his comforts, his dog, and his wife and feel that they are his. And the husband came to think that all the wife wanted was a place from which she could step out with more security than that of her unmarried women friends. Though overdrawn, the picture revealed the possessiveness which seems to "come naturally" to conventional marital love.

But when love is the fruit of the Spirit, possessiveness is transformed into trusteeship. Jesus enunciated a principle whose profundity has not been sufficiently appreciated by the pulpit. ". . . if you have not been faithful in that which is another's, who will give you that which is your own?"[8] We get what belongs to our full self-realization by first being faithful trustees of what belongs to others. If a person enters marital union with the thought of perquisites for himself, he is bound erelong to question its profitableness. But if he devotes himself to safeguarding the interests of his wife and children, he feels enriched by the dividends of family love.

Godly love is not jealous or boastful because it is free from pride and possessiveness. It does not make me look upon my beloved as belonging to me but makes me feel that I belong to her. It keeps me from boasting of the prize which I have won by causing me to feel humbly grateful for my undeserved good fortune.

LOVE IS "NOT ARROGANT OR RUDE"   The old saying, "All's fair in love and war," carries the implication that love-making is a contest between competitors and the end justifies the means. Such a concept gives scope for arrogance and rudeness in the making of love, and screen interpretations of romance sometimes suggest the superior effectiveness of rough methods.

And how easily arrogance can creep into family circles. When persons of unequal talent and tempo are teamed together, the quicker-minded is prone to show a rude impatience toward the slower-witted, and the stronger is likely to exhibit a condescending stoop toward the weaker. To ignore the views, to interrupt the conversation, to criticize in the presence of company—many are the ways in which rudeness mars the romance of marriage and the parent-child relationship. Many a husband and father, frustrated by his lack of achievement in the competitive world outside the home, finds outlet for his repressed egoism within the family circle. Many a less-talented layman, feeling his ambition thwarted in business, arrogantly throws his weight around in church circles.

But when love is the fruit of the Spirit, it is gentle. Consider Paul himself. He was anything but gentle by nature. As a young man he was so violently defensive of his religious convictions that when he heard a new sect was threatening the faith of his fathers he went

---

[8] Luke 16:12.

around "breathing threats and murder" against it.[9] He was present at the stoning of the Christian martyr Stephen and held the garments of those who did the stoning. But after his soul-shaking experience on the Damascus road and the long painful meditation and ministration which followed, Paul discovered that "the fruit of the Spirit is love, joy, peace, patience, kindness, goodness, faithfulness, gentleness, self-control."[1]

Godly love develops that "fineness of nature" which John Ruskin declared to be the chief mark of a gentleman. It makes a person sensitively considerate of the secret wishes and the modestly concealed merits of others. It begets a kind of good taste in human relationships which detects unfairness as an artist feels a clash of colors in the décor of a room. Love born of the Spirit imparts a sympathetic understanding to home circles where members can unpack their hearts with words, where listening love sifts the wheat from the chaff of chatter and goes on caring for the speaker, where shy little wallflowers blossom out and the less brilliant members of the household do not bury their single talent in a napkin because of an inferiority complex.

The godly home is the most fertile soil for the growing of reverence. Randolph Miller of Yale asserts that reverence is caught rather than taught. It may dawn on a child to be reverent because of the manner in which grace is said at table. Another child may learn it from the way his mother cares for the flowers in the garden. But chiefly, says Professor Miller, we learn reverence for the Lord from the mutual concern manifested among members of the family. "When I have been forgiven, when my loneliness is overcome, when my relationships with other persons are stable and healthy and strong, when I realize love that I do not deserve—then I am thankful in my reverence."[2]

LOVE "DOES NOT INSIST ON ITS OWN WAY"   While our natures are made for love and cannot be fulfilled without it, they are not ready-made

---

[9] Acts 9:1.

[1] Galatians 5:22–23.

[2] Randolph Crump Miller, "The Education of Christians," *The Pulpit,* March 1956, p. 6.

for love. We must all undergo some alterations if we are successfully to enter any relationship of love, whether it be family, friendship, community, or church. As individuals we get "set in our ways" and at a surprisingly early age. We crave love but we are prone to be too prescriptive as well as too possessive.

There are two statements of Jesus which are strikingly suggestive when set in juxtaposition. On one occasion the disciples came to him and said, "Master, we saw a man casting out demons in your name, and we forbade him, because he does not follow with us." Jesus replied, "Do not forbid him; for he that is not against you is for you."[3]

At another time Jesus, observing the tactics of the Pharisees, declared: "He who is not with me is against me, and he who does not gather with me scatters."[4]

These two statements, viewed together, reveal that Jesus was concerned with spirit more than method, with purpose more than label, with direction more than definition. The other healer whom the disciples restrained was headed in the direction of helpfulness. Toward him Christ's followers should be tolerant and inclusive. The Pharisee critics, on the other hand, were obstructionists. While Jesus in the spirit of love was a gathering force, they in the spirit of hate were scattering. The goal of love is togetherness. The Christian is to be firm in facing toward that goal. He is not to be narrow in insisting on his own way of reaching it.

Love cultivated in godliness distinguishes between appeasement and adjustment. Appeasement is the effort, sometimes selfish in motive and obsequious in manner, to placate the feelings and satisfy the desires of the other party. A parent may try to appease a child by catering to his whims and tantrums. The effect may be as disastrous to the character of the child as Neville Chamberlain's effort at appeasement was to the peace of Europe. Godly good will does not sacrifice principle for the sake of a transient peace but it does scrap preconceived notions and prefabricated programs in order to approach just agreements.

True love tries to keep its influence as free as possible from inter-

---

[3] Luke 9:49–50.
[4] Luke 11:23.

ference. Like the divine Spirit portrayed in Revelation, love stands at the door of its beloved and knocks but it does not barge in on the other's privacy. A good mother yearns to help her daughter in some acute problem of the girl's new home but wisely refrains from interfering. Trite but true is the adage that we are to be our brother's brother and not our brother's keeper.

Godly love does not count on argument to secure the spirit of unity. Differences are dissolved not in words but in common loyalties. When husband John says to wife Mary: "Now, Mary, be reasonable. Let's sit down and argue this out," it is not at all certain that either Mary or John will be calmly reasonable. But if they get to thinking about their children, whose love they both cherish and to whom they both want to be loyal, their differences are likely to lose their tension. When differences arise in our family relationships, we do not argue ourselves into believing the same thing, but we love ourselves into believing in each other. Love does not demand that all parties see eye to eye. I should imagine it would be dull business living with a life partner who always agreed with me, although I have not verified this by experience!

When love is the fruit of the Spirit, it does not insist on its own way but on seeking God's way.

LOVE IS "NOT IRRITABLE OR RESENTFUL" Degrees of irritability differ with temperament and fluctuate with physical health. Some persons are by nature more quick-tempered than others. On some days all of us are more sensitive to irritation than at other times. Temper is a strange but necessary ingredient of our natures. If we "show our temper" that is bad. If we "lose our temper" that is also bad. It is a quality which gives strength and stability to human nature, when in the right proportion and under the proper control. Temper is to man's nature somewhat as temper is to steel. Crude iron has to be properly tempered to acquire the fine edge and flexibility of steel.

Healthy mature love is the result of divine tempering. It has been said that hot-tempered persons make the best saints. The gospels record that James and John in a fit of temper were eager to call down fire from heaven and consume a certain village which refused

a welcome to the disciples.[5] Yet tradition has it that the hot-
tempered John was transformed into the most tender and loving
member of the apostolic company. Strong feelings which may flare
up into flaming passion can generate emotional power when properly controlled.

A person is not good for much unless, as we say, he has the fire
in him. But his worth depends on whether the fire takes the form
of hotheadedness or warmheartedness. Saul of Tarsus, "breathing
threats and murder" against the Christian enemies of his Hebrew
faith,[6] was so tempered in the furnace of experience that he bade
his readers "be aglow with the Spirit, serve the Lord."[7] When heat
of passion is changed into glow of spirit, love is maturing.

When love is cultivated with godliness, it grows above the pettiness of irritability. We allow little pinpricks to "get under our skin."
We ought to be ashamed of it, and in our better moods we do blush
for our weaker moments. God imparts a high-mindedness which
overlooks low-lying irritations. He begets a magnanimity of spirit
which takes a big view of tense situations and gives the benefit of
the doubt when motives are in question. It was said of Lincoln that
he never forgot a favor or remembered an insult.

While irritability causes the painful flashes of temper, resentment
is deeper. It sinks into a sullenness which smolders and poisons the
spirit. Love as it matures becomes increasingly master of moods. We
may discuss our moods as little weaknesses rather than sins, but they
do play havoc with the health and happiness of ourselves and others.
I think of a teacher who suffered deep wrong in her own life, yet
bravely concealed her depressed feelings lest any mood of resentment should cast a shadow on the minds of her pupils. To be master
of our moods is a mark of love's triumph.

But such victorious love needs divine cultivation. It requires the
grace of forgiveness, which also has the gift of being able to forget.
Just as the vergers of great cathedrals are said to acquire a dignity
of bearing by working under the lofty arches, so the godly man de-

---

[5] Luke 9:54.
[6] Acts 9:1.
[7] Romans 12:11.

velops an equanimity of spirit and a spaciousness of sympathy by living as a child of the gracious Heavenly Father who "makes his sun rise on the evil and on the good, and sends rain on the just and on the unjust."[8]

LOVE "DOES NOT REJOICE AT WRONG, BUT REJOICES IN THE RIGHT" Perhaps Moffatt puts this description of love even better: "Love is never glad when others go wrong but is eager to believe the best." A minister once went to comfort a man who was in deep sorrow over the loss of his son. The burden of the caller's conversation was the sufferings and hardships of their mutual friends. The minister meant well but he was striking the wrong chord. The self-centeredness of our natures is reflected in the fact that we are prone to console ourselves by comparisons with those who are worse off. To be sure, we should be grateful that we have been spared calamities which have come to others, but love that is of God finds sorrow rather than comfort in the sufferings of others.

It is a strain of sinfulness in our natures which makes us eager to read about the foibles, the sins, the crimes of others. Yet our newsstands reveal how deep-seated is this trait. The parading of human weaknesses in the press is often explained by saying that only bad deeds are exceptional enough to make news. While there is some truth in the statement, let us not take too much credit from the thought that goodness is too common to be reported. The sad fact is that human nature is bad enough to enjoy bad news.

Added to this weakness is another—that of excusing our own sins by looking at the shortcomings of others. The Corinthians to whom Paul was writing were exhibiting this weakness: "When they measure themselves by one another, and compare themselves with one another, they are without understanding."[9] Like the Corinthians, we are prone to create a clublike atmosphere of mutual exoneration. We may beguile ourselves into thinking that a soft tolerance of others' weaknesses is a sign of our broad-mindedness, even of our brotherly love, whereas in fact it is only a revelation of our own self-interest.

Love ripened in godliness does not find consolation in the suffer-

---

[8] Matthew 5:45.
[9] 2 Corinthians 10:12.

ings of others nor does it find secret satisfaction in the shortcomings of others. The godly man is a well-wisher. He is glad when others succeed. He rejoices when his neighbors go right. He is eager to believe the best. He looks for "whatever is true, whatever is honorable, whatever is just, whatever is pure, whatever is lovely, whatever is gracious."[1] He looks for the footprints of the good and the great rather than for the fingerprints of the plotting and the perverse. Thus he keeps his mind from being overcome with evil and depressed by suspicion and fear. He realizes that evil is the absence of love as darkness is the absence of light. As the darkness is driven out of the room by letting in the light, so evil is banished not by the fist and the sword but by letting in the light of love. And this light must be more than the flashlight of fleeting, self-generated, so-called natural love. It must be the pervading and persistent sunlight of divine love.

"So faith, hope, love abide, these three; but the greatest of these is love."[2] This triumvirate must rule together because they abide together. No one of them can endure without the other two. The first commandment to love God is linked with the second commandment to love one's neighbor, for they stand or fall together.

---

[1] Philippians 4:8.
[2] 1 Corinthians 13:13.

9 OUR LOVING ENEMIES

Foes within the Family
Saved from Our Friends
"Leave Us Not to Ourselves"

A radio listener wrote these words: "My mother, of whom I was very fond, recently passed away. Turning to the Bible for comfort, I ran across this passage: 'If any one comes to me and does not hate his own father and mother and wife and children and brothers and sisters, yes, and even his own life, he cannot be my disciple.'[1] How am I to understand such seemingly inhuman words coming from Jesus?"

The writer speaks for many puzzled readers. Hate is an emotion alien to the spirit of Jesus. How can he who bade us love our enemies command us to hate our loved ones?

We can imagine a monk or bitter recluse advocating a distrust and denial of family affection. But Jesus was no aloof ascetic. He entered so vivaciously into human relationships that he was a welcome guest at wedding feasts. He was so interested in little children that he invited them to him and was so interesting to them that they came. That he should speak of hating the members of one's own family is hard to believe.

We turn to the translation for light. When Matthew reports this saying of Jesus, he makes it sound somewhat less harsh: "He who loves father or mother more than me is not worthy of me; and he who loves son or daughter more than me is not worthy of me."[2] Yet while Matthew thus softens Jesus' words, his record still puzzles, for he interprets Our Lord as saying in the same context: "Do not think that I have come to bring peace on earth; I have not come to bring peace, but a sword. For I have come to set a man against his father,

---

[1] Luke 14:26.
[2] Matthew 10:37.

and a daughter against her mother, and a daughter-in-law against her mother-in-law; and a man's foes will be those of his own household."[3]

To be sure, we Western readers must make some allowance for oriental hyperbole. Jesus and the New Testament writers put many of their ideas in extravagant and paradoxical form to arrest attention.

Also we must take account of the tense conditions under which Christ's first followers lived. The converts to his cause were often ostracized by their families. They risked persecution, even martyrdom. Emperor Julian with sarcastic humor said that, since Christians believed they must be poor to enter the kingdom of Heaven, the government would help them toward their goal by confiscating their property. We can well understand how under such conditions families would be divided by the new Christian movement. If one member of a family felt the call of Christ, he might endanger the safety of the whole household by following. Understandably the early Christians frequently had to choose between loyalty to family and commitment to Christ.

Foes within the Family

Nevertheless, after making allowance for oriental language and apostolic persecution, we confront a basic principle: Jesus Christ insisted that his followers recognize a sovereign love and loyalty. The first command is, "You shall love the Lord your God," and the first loyalty is, ". . . seek first his kingdom and his righteousness."[1] Whenever any love or interest conflicts with this sovereignty, it is looked upon as hostile, even though it be in behalf of those nearest and dearest to us.

Consider how a man could have foes in his own household. Jesus was made familiar in his boyhood with such a beautiful home life that when he came to portray God the best picture he could give was that of Father. He breathed the air of family loyalty so characteristic of the Hebrew people. He stressed the Mosaic command, "Honor your father and your mother."[2] One of his last words from

[3] Matthew 10:34–36.
[1] Matthew 6:33.
[2] Exodus 20:12.

the cross concerned the care of his mother. Jesus was well aware that a man's home is his castle of security, to which he turns when buffeted by the world. How he missed the home from which his ministry called him was revealed in his poignant words: "Foxes have holes, and birds of the air have nests; but the Son of man has nowhere to lay his head."[3] When we have spent ourselves in the strain of a competitive society where men are trying to *get* the best of us, how blessed it is to come back to a circle of love where others are trying to *make* the best of us. Jesus made clear that he knew all this.

Nevertheless, Jesus detected the dangers which lurk in the very comforts and kindnesses of the home circle. Loved ones can often become our foes by being too protective. If Jesus had heeded the wishes of his own family, he would have followed a safe course and remained a popular teacher in Galilee. Recall the occasion on which his disciples came to him and announced that his mother and brothers were waiting outside the place in which he was speaking. Jesus answered that announcement with a statement which seems cold and enigmatic. He said: "Who is my mother, and who are my brothers?" And looking about on the listeners around him, he added: "Here are my mother and my brothers! For whoever does the will of my Father in heaven is my brother, and sister, and mother."[4] In this striking manner Jesus resisted the request of his own family to cease his dangerous public duties and return to the safety of private life.

We have become so obsessed with young people as problems that we sometimes forget that they can be prophets. Parents should remember that they can learn from their children as well as teach them. The little child sometimes has a freshness of insight and a purity of mind which parents need to get. And it still happens that a high sense of duty may drive a son or daughter, as it drove Jesus, to go beyond the family pattern. A half century ago a sixteen-year-old youth in Japan joined an English Bible class taught by an American Christian missionary. The boy came from a wealthy, aristocratic Japanese family. His uncle desired for him a diplomatic career. But the atmosphere of his home was heavy and the lad was restless. He

---

[3] Matthew 8:20.
[4] Matthew 12:48–50.

became imbued with the Christlike spirit of service and began to
teach in a Sunday school. His uncle disinherited him and he went
without funds to a theological seminary in Kobe. He began to preach
and teach in a slum district. That youth was Kagawa, later the most
significant Japanese Christian leader.

In our American churches the Christian faith has been presented
as so conventional and congenial that we seldom think of it as causing
the sacrifice of home ties. But when Christ is taken to heart, he may
create a situation which breaks the heart. "Think not," said Christ,
"that I am come to bring peace"—that is, in the form we call peace
of mind. His coming may bring the sword of the spirit. But the testimony of experience is that Christ's sword cuts with healing surgery.

Our loved ones become our foes in many less dramatic ways than
those depicted in apostolic times. Some years ago a novelist pictured
a wife who got the impression that her husband was being imposed
upon in his work at the office. She warned him repeatedly against
letting others put their burdens on him. She dropped the idea into
his mind as regularly as she put the sugar into his breakfast coffee.
After a time this affected his way of thinking and made him feel
that he was a fool to exert himself too much. Then, in a kind of
marital reciprocity, he began to beg her not to tax herself in service
to others. Thus the two nursed themselves into soft selfishness.

Contrast that woman's weakening influence with the spirit of
Wendell Phillips' wife. The latter was an invalid. Every night before
Phillips went out to speak for the slavery reforms so dear to his heart
and so dangerous to his reputation, he would go to his wife's bedside. She would take his hand in both of hers and say, "Don't
shilly-shally tonight, Wendell!" Such fortifying influence is beyond
measure.

Recently the president of a great corporation told the Los Angeles
Rotary Club that "business doesn't hire men, it hires families." He
meant that the worker's home life is a vital factor in his technical
efficiency and producing power. But in the 1930s when Germany
was yielding to the pressures of Hitlerism, Sinclair Lewis wrote a
book called *It Can't Happen Here*, in which he showed how subtly
individual resistance to heroic policies can be weakened by the

thought, "I have a wife and family to support." The home circle can soften as well as strengthen.

Our natural personal loves, beautiful as they are, need larger loyalties to keep them healthy. There is point to the poetic line,

> I could not love thee, dear, so much,
> Loved I not honor more.

Husband and wife cannot preserve wholesome affection by devoting themselves to each other exclusively. When two persons set out with no higher interest than that of looking after each other, the relationship resembles the childish sport of teeter-totter. When one is down, the other must be up, and the watching of the other's ups and downs grows tiresome and trivial. When love in the home would soften us by its protectiveness and limit us by its possessiveness, then "a man's foes are those of his own household."

Saved from Our Friends

This well-meant weakening may also invade the circle of friendship. Friends stand between a person and the hard contacts of the street, serving to break the shock of bad news and to share the satisfactions of good fortune. Without friends even the strongest individual finds life too exposed for long endurance.

Jesus showed his awareness of this fact. He craved the comradeship of his intimate circle. During his last trying week in Jerusalem he found respite from the fickle and hostile crowds in the restoring company of his closest friends at Bethany. And at his Last Supper he said gratefully to his disciples, "You are those who have continued with me in my trials."[1]

Yet Jesus also detected the dangers which lurk in friendship. Just about the sharpest words of rebuke he ever spoke were uttered to his devoted disciple Peter, and at a time when the latter was trying to be kind to him. When Jesus announced that he must go up to Jerusalem and suffer the worst at the hands of his enemies, Peter protested, saying, "God forbid, Lord! This shall never happen to you." Although Peter's protest was prompted by love, Jesus said to him, "Get behind me, Satan! You are a hindrance to me; for you are

---

[1] Luke 22:28.

not on the side of God, but of men."[2] Why such sharp language? The resemblance of Jesus' words to those recorded of the wilderness temptation might lead us to think that the Master was speaking to himself, even more than to Peter. Was Peter at this moment giving voice to the secret desires of Jesus' own heart? Here at Caesarea Philippi, as later in Gethsemane, Jesus' sensitive nature shrank from the torture of the cross.

We cannot presume to read Jesus' mind in that remark, but we know how often friends do voice the unspoken desires of our own minds. Their sympathetic minds are the sounding boards which reinforce the echoes of what we are saying to ourselves. Thus friends may comfort us. Our companions may be those to whom we go in order to have our consciences quieted rather than disturbed, those to whom we turn to save our faces rather than to save our souls.

One of the most difficult lessons in friendship is to learn how to mix criticism with appreciation in the proper proportion to produce a tonic rather than a sedative. In *The Bridge of San Luis Rey* Thornton Wilder depicted with penetrating insight the relationship between a popular concert-hall singer and her discoverer and tutor, Uncle Pio. The singer was quite content with mediocre work provided she received the crowd's applause. But after each performance she had to face her Pygmalion, Uncle Pio, who was standing in the wings.

As that music teacher stood behind the stage keeping watch over his ward, so the Christ stands in the wings of life's stage to keep his followers from being too easily content when the crowd is friendly and from being too depressed when the crowd is hostile. Our friends become our loving enemies when they leave us satisfied with our second best. When Katherine Mansfield was being congratulated by some of her friends on certain of her poems, she exclaimed, "There isn't one of them I can show to God!" Her clear and honest mind heard the call of a higher voice than that of her friends.

"Leave Us Not to Ourselves"
Left to itself, the love that comes naturally loses its lifting power.

---

[2] Matthew 16:22–23.

Love has to be stretched to keep its resiliency. William James wrote wisely when he advised doing at least one unpleasant duty every day to keep in moral trim. A young woman came to Henry Link, the late well-recognized psychologist, complaining that she was depressed with loneliness. Her circle of friendship was shrinking to imprisoning proportions. Probing into her history, Link found that she had made a practice of mingling only with persons she liked. If company came to her home, she would let the rest of the family entertain them unless she was fond of them. By never putting herself out for others, she found herself less and less taken in by others.

A few years ago a prominent Negro minister in a Lenten service prayed, "O Lord, leave us not to ourselves." His petition set my mind thinking back along the line of his race's history. His ancestors stemmed from the African jungle. What if God had left them there? Many white persons are saying that the Negro race would have been much happier if left in its African habitat. Pulpits have even found scriptural support for such a view in the words of St. Paul at Athens: "[God] made from one every nation of men to live on all the face of the earth, having determined allotted periods and the boundaries of their habitation."[1] But the Bible advocates no divine *apartheid*. This is one world designed as the dwelling of the one and whole family of God. Ungodly beyond words were the slave trade and commercial exploitation which disturbed the African Negroes in their homeland, but certainly it was not God's purpose to keep the races separate by permanent geographical partitions. "Here there cannot be Greek and Jew, circumcised and uncircumcised, barbarian, Scythian, slave, free man, but Christ is all, and in all."[2]

It is the selfishness in us and not the love in us which desires to be left undisturbed by differences, even by tensions. Mark records the man with the "unclean spirit" crying out, "What have you to do with us, Jesus of Nazareth? Have you come to destroy us?"[3] The presence of Christ is as disturbing to the smug, the complacent, the self-centered as heat is at first to the man sinking into a freezing

---

[1] Acts 17:26.
[2] Colossians 3:11.
[3] Mark 1:24.

numbness. With the application of heat comes pain but it is the pain of returning vigor.

"I have not come to bring peace, but a sword," said the Christ.[4] There is pain in godly love, sometimes the ache of loneliness, or the burning of desire, or the hurt of others' wounds. But these are life's growing pains. And those who would keep us from growing by sparing us from pain are our loving enemies.

---

[4] Matthew 10:34.

The Acid Test of Love

Dr. Ray Lyman Wilbur was wont to say that, when he presented a proposition to his faculty at Leland Stanford University and received unanimous consent, he knew that he was ten years too late. Any original and significant proposal always arouses some opposition.

We can well imagine the dark looks of disagreement which greeted Jesus' words when he said: "You have heard that it was said, 'You shall love your neighbor and hate your enemy.' But I say to you, Love your enemies and pray for those who persecute you."[1] Jesus was speaking to a people living in an occupied country under the heel of hated Roman legions. They were looking for a Messiah to lift the galling yoke of subservience. To advocate love for the enemies of their country smacked of treason, and to expect it savored of insanity.

After nineteen centuries this command of the Christ still strikes the majority of his so-called followers as an impossible counsel of perfection and in time of war as subversive doctrine. Religious fundamentalists, who assert their belief in "every word of the Bible from cover to cover," seem to overlook these words of Jesus when they angrily attack the "heretical" teachings of those churchmen who disagree with them. And if a parish preacher were to advocate love for the enemies of his country during war, unless he watered his sermon down to the thin soup of pious platitudes, some of his members might walk out of the service and many would withdraw their support.

---

[1] Matthew 5:43-44.

It has been the thesis of this book that Jesus linked the two commands of love for God and love for neighbor because they stand or fall together. And if it is impossible to "love your neighbor as yourself" without loving God with all your heart, certainly it is futile to talk of love for enemies without divine help. Jesus seemed clearly to imply this, for his command is: "Love your enemies and pray for those who persecute you, so that you may be sons of your Father who is in heaven; for he makes his sun rise on the evil and on the good, and sends rain on the just and on the unjust."[2] Only in the consciousness of God's grace and in co-operation with his spirit is there hope of meeting the acid test of love, which is love for enemies.

Who Are Our Enemies?

For one thing God helps us to see who our enemies are. It is very probable that every one of us looks upon certain persons as enemies, whereas those individuals are not conscious of any hostility toward us. Conversely we are no doubt regarded as hostile by some individuals toward whom we feel no enmity whatsoever. Something said or done may have been misinterpreted as an unfriendly act, or false rumor may have reached ears hidden from our sight. Thus some of our "enemies" may be the creation of imagination and misinformation, and what is needed for our wounded feelings is the septic healing of truth.

Yonder is a little boy, tear-stained of face and bitter in heart, who thinks his father is his enemy because the parent has denied him a cherished desire. Yet that father yearns to remove the misunderstanding and convince the lad of his love. Many adult enmities are almost equally childish. The late Dwight Morrow, speaking out of his experience in business leadership and international diplomacy, declared that we judge others by their actions and ourselves by our ideals. Because of this proneness we are bidden by Our Lord, "Judge not, that you be not judged."[1] To be sure, we do judge actions and it is difficult not to project our judgment into the realm of motives behind the deeds, but in doing so we should ever be aware

---

[2] Matthew 5:44–45.
[1] Matthew 7:1.

of our partial knowledge. It is the part of worldly wisdom never to impute to others motives lower than our own. And when wisdom is illumined with godly love, it believes the best until it helps to bring out the best.

We say that love is blind. Sometimes it does see dimly. But hate and fear are more nearly blind. There are periods when people fool themselves by believing too much. But it is also possible to be fooled by believing too little. And that is the more prevalent danger in this time when propagandists flourish so prosperously. It is easier to play on people's fears and hatreds than on their confidence and love. Propaganda seems to need the "anti" note to make its appeal. Columnists and commentators have discovered this. The pulpit often echoes the street in stirring up suspicion rather than sympathy. We are living in a defensive mood. We have pulled down the visors of our faith and take only low views of men and events. Believing the worst about other persons and peoples, we tend to call forth their worst. When a person knows that he is under suspicion, he is likely to do unnatural things which make him still more suspect. Thus distrust begets distrust and, unless checked, leads to disaster.

When we set our fears and feelings of enmity in the light of God through prayer, we first of all seek the truth as to the real identity of our enemies. We distinguish between truth seeking and mere fact finding. Ill will is being fomented by propagandists who marshal facts to prove their pet theories. Good will can and must be generated by those who seek the truth, lead where it may, cost what it will. It is not easy to find the truth in a world as complex and cloudy and curtained off as ours. But one thing the godly person can do is to clean the lens of his own vision from falsehoods, hatreds, and filming fancy.

Why Are They Our Enemies?

A second thing is done for us when we "pray for those who persecute us." We are helped to see why they are our enemies. While we cannot with certainty judge their motives, we can see more clearly how we look to them. Jesus warned against the tendency to complain that others misunderstand us. He said: "Why do you see the speck that is in your brother's eye, but do not notice the log that is in your own eye? Or how can you say to your brother, 'Let me take the speck out of your eye,' when there is the log in your own eye? You hypocrite, first take the log out of your own eye, and then you will see clearly to take the speck out of your brother's eye."[1] The pointed irony of this passage runs the gamut from the husband who excuses himself by saying that his wife does not understand him up to the nations on both sides of the Iron Curtain who complain that their motives are misunderstood and maligned by the peoples on the other side of the screen.

With Bobby Burns we should pray:

Oh wad some power the giftie gie us
To see oursels as others see us.

We Americans, for example, convince *ourselves* that we desire no foreign territory, that we shall never use our vast power to hurt any other nation unless it attacks us. But do we convince others? As I write this page, I am in Spain. Our government is spending vast sums to establish air bases in Spain. Our policy makers sincerely believe that those bases will help to safeguard the free world and at the same time benefit the unstable economy of Spain. But many a Spaniard believes that America is establishing these military outposts because she prefers the next war, if it comes, to be fought on territory other than her own. We of America feel that such Spanish opinion is unjust and unfounded, but are we fully aware how easy it is for the man on the Madrid street to misunderstand our motives?

It would be well to recall some words spoken by Edmund Burke to his countrymen in 1793 regarding England's policy toward France: "I must fairly say that I dread our own power and our own ambition. . . . We may say that we shall not abuse this astonishing and hitherto unheard of power. But every nation will think we shall abuse it. . . . Sooner or later this state of things must produce a combination against us which may end in our ruin."[2]

Burke's words should cause us in America to look with searching insight into the way other nations view our vast strength and the

---

[1] Matthew 7:3–5.

[2] Quoted in H. J. Morgenthau, *Politics among Nations* (New York, 1954), pp. 121–22.

resentment which naturally rises at the sight of our unmatched wealth. We naturally resent the criticism of countries which we have helped with our bounty. But we shall make matters worse if our reaction is to close our purses rather than to open our minds.

We need to set our personal and national misunderstandings in the sight of God's rule in order to see realistically. The causes of world ferment are not all to be blamed on communism. Some of the global unrest is due to the means of communication which now enable undeveloped peoples to see how the privileged countries live. Some of the yeasty restlessness is due to the spirit of Christianity, which has been disturbing men with divine discontent in the presence of injustice, disease, poverty, and repression. Yet, seeing all this, we must not blind ourselves to the unchristian motivation of communism. Badly as reforms are needed, let us not repeat the mistake of calling the communists mere "agrarian reformers." Communism is a cruel program of proposed cure by class strife, which is at the opposite pole from the Christian doctrine of reform through love for one's neighbor, even for one's enemy.

We cannot see our complex world realistically from the sidewalk level. Our improved means of communication do not suffice to create mutual understanding. We demand an impossible service from our newspapers and radio. If anything significant happens today in Singapore or South Africa, we expect our press and radio to give us the news by tonight or tomorrow morning. They may report external facts, but to interpret the meaning of events they must generalize in order to cover the world stage. And naturally the generalization comes through government spokesmen. If the White House or Congress speaks, the rest of the world says, "That is America talking." If Downing Street speaks, the world says, "That is Britain's view." When the Kremlin speaks, other nations conclude that is what Russia thinks. But America is more than the White House and Congress. Great Britain is more than Downing Street and even in the monolithic Soviet Union there are feelings and forces to be reckoned with outside the Kremlin, as instanced by the growing inquisitiveness of students and the popularity of American pianists. If we are ever to have an approximation of world understanding, there must be viewers and voices beyond the political spokesmen.

At this point religion is called to render a service supplementing secular communication. Even more than information, society needs Christlike imagination. Cold facts may make cold wars. Our need is to see the human emotions beyond the economic formulae, the family situations behind the governmental fronts. Our imaginations must be sensitized to see how life looks to lads whose future is frustrated by a dictator's whims or a flimsy national economy and to parents who hear their little children crying themselves to sleep with hunger. It is my belief that by and large the women of America are using more imagination in viewing the contemporary world than are the men. In their missionary societies and women's clubs they are giving more persistent study to the personal aspects of world problems. When we sincerely pray for those on the other side of dividing issues and curtains, we catch new insights into their feelings about their own situation and into their understanding of ourselves.

Yes, and our religion should help us to see more clearly into the meaning of events. "The part of Christian belief is to provide insight, [which] is of crucial significance for living. . . . William James remarked . . . 'When we see all things in God and refer all things to Him, we read in common matters superior expressions of meaning. . . .' Here is the essence of the relationship of Christian insight to the data of liberal education. In every concrete fact and temporal event there is potential meaning that beggars the imagination. A liberal education does not reach its own goal unless a student senses something of this meaning."[3]

How Magnanimous Can We Be?

Moreover, prayer not only sets our enmities in the clearer light of truth but it also brings them into the atmosphere of God's magnanimity and love. We look up to a Father who "makes his sun rise on the evil and on the good, and sends rain on the just and on the unjust."[1] Our thoughts are turned from resentment at what others are trying to do *to* us to gratitude for what God has done *for* us. When we ponder God's magnanimous generosity and forgiving grace, we

---

[3] E. Harrison Harbison in *The Christian Idea of Education* (New Haven, 1957), p. 76.
[1] Matthew 5:45.

are shamed out of our little-mindedness and petty grudges. It is our pigmy enmities and suspicions that more commonly get us down. Few nervous breakdowns are caused by fear of war with the Soviet Union or other world calamities. It is the little meannesses and envies and jealousies which creep into the cracks of life and send us to the psychiatrists. Books on world peace are read by the thoughtful few. Books on peace of mind dealing with little irritations and discontents become best sellers. The contagion of God's great-mindedness is a needed and overlooked element of cure for our be-deviling discontents, anxieties, and divisiveness.

We are familiar with the fruitful results of magnanimity when it is manifested in intimate and personal relations. The wife or friend who magnanimously forgives thaws out the icicled springs of the cold heart and opens the channels of the mind to the joy of making up. The manifestation of magnanimity by great individuals illumines history with bright spots. During the struggle between the North and the South in America, General Robert E. Lee was severely criticized by a colleague, General Whiting. A day came when President Jefferson Davis of the Confederacy summoned Lee for consultation and asked his opinion of General Whiting. Lee commended his critic as an able officer. Another officer who was present pulled Lee aside later and asked him if he did not know of the unkind things which Whiting had said about him. Lee replied that he was aware of them but he understood that President Davis desired to know what he thought of Whiting and not what Whiting thought of him. Examples of such magnanimity exert an ennobling influence.

It would, of course, be naïve to assert that governments can be magnanimous in quite the same way as individuals. It is one thing to overlook an injury done to myself, it is another to overlook a wrong done to one for whom I am responsible. Governments are responsible for citizens within their borders, and in our present interrelated world they must also share responsibility for the welfare of the people beyond their borders. A Christian individual may convert his adversary by obeying Christ's injunction: ". . . if any one forces you to go one mile, go with him two miles."[2] Thus was Jean Valjean's

---

[2] Matthew 5:41.

heart changed by the generous and forgiving bishop whose candle-stick he had stolen. But a responsible government, though it represents a "Christian nation," cannot magnanimously forgive the marauder who robs the property of its citizens or rapes a Czechoslovakia or despoils a Hungary. Magnanimity is not a virtue which can be manifested vicariously as was done at Munich.

Christian idealists often overlook this point in advocating peace measures. They fail to differentiate in applying Christ's ethics to individuals and to governments and thus bring their theories into disrepute as fanciful dreams. On the other hand, spokesmen of the church often fail to inject any distinctively Christian note into political discussion. Conferences of churchmen on world peace are frequently difficult to distinguish from conferences of political economists. The church is called to be the conscience of the state, and a good conscience listens to the voice of God above the confusion of mere practical calculations.

When we lift governmental ethics up into the light of God, we can cite some historical situations in which magnanimous attitudes proved their effectiveness, as witness the Boxer Indemnity and the liberation of the Philippines. In India, I have heard the saying that after the British were ejected from the front door they came around to the back door to serve their former colonials. Appreciation of this attitude is shown by the people of India in many ways.

And the rising spirit of nationalism which is so divisive should not cause Christians to discount the value of their foreign missionary service. The century-long sending of faithful missionaries, interested in individuals as persons, not as pawns, has left reservoirs of good will throughout the world. Let us not allow the word "mission" to lose its Christian connotation. Today, when we speak of America sending a "mission" to Pakistan or South Vietnam, it usually means a company of military experts to advise on defense. Christianity is our best defense against communism, provided we use it to promote love and service and not merely to save us from the Soviets.

In the summer of 1957 a British newspaper startled at least one American visitor with the headline that the United States did not plan her foreign policy to make friends but to defend her own interests. Apparently the impression emanated from the efforts of

America's Secretary of State to placate a congressional committee which was opposed to foreign aid. The irate congressmen had to be convinced that money spent abroad was to advance America rather than to help less developed nations. Certainly in such a spirit, "the gift without the giver is bare." At least, when we look at other nations in the light of God's love, we are lifted above "enlightened self-interest." Enlightened self-interest is never enlightened enough when man alone does the lighting.

How Sovereign Is a Nation?

We turn to God for help in loving our enemies for still a fourth reason. He shows us our dependence on the other members of his family. To secure our desired independence within the framework of our dependence is a task too great for man's own wisdom and strength, as we have seen in the circles near to us.

Turn now to the larger realm of nations, both friendly and hostile. The President of the United States salutes no foreign ruler, for no other nation holds authority over us. The only object which the head of our government salutes is the flag, and he salutes that as the symbol of the sovereign people. Yet when the so-called sovereign people elect a President, they require him to take his oath or affirmation on the Bible, thus symbolizing the recognition of a power higher than the officer elected or the citizens who elect. We open our national legislatures with prayer, thus acknowledging the existence of divine moral laws undergirding the statutes made by man. And recently we have incorporated into the salute to the flag the words "under God." Both explicitly and symbolically we assert that America is a "nation under God."

This assertion implies that our government's laws and acts are tested by our best judgments of God's standards. It means that loyalty to our country involves trying to keep America loyal to God. Yet, like other nations, the United States is determined to safeguard its own sovereignty. We are ever being warned against the danger of surrendering our sovereignty in organizations and programs of international co-operation. But if this is a world "under God," it follows that no individual or nation can enjoy absolute sovereignty. No man can be complete lord of himself, for "no man liveth unto himself." We can live together in families and communities only as we limit our own sovereignty.

The time has come to lift our sights from the personal and national level to the international scene. When the United States assumed leadership in the Atomic Energy Commission, it expressed its willingness to limit its sovereignty in certain specific ways, recognizing that adequate international control of atomic energy would require similar action by all nations. In nuclear weapons man has taken hold of forces too big for any one nation to handle. No nation can be the sole judge of its right to use these titanic new powers. To be sure, we must preserve our fullest possible freedom as a nation. But as Dr. A. William Loos of the Church Peace Union puts it, "We have to consider ways in which a self-limitation upon the exercise of our sovereignty may help to make more effective those international measures that are directed against war and toward a freer world community."

Just as a person fulfills himself through co-operation in a family, so a nation fulfills itself through co-operation in the family of nations. We must test under God the holding of our so-called sovereignty.

And when we do look at our nation as a member of God's family, we see not only the necessity of co-operation but also the blessings of it. We Americans are so prone to think that world co-operation puts us always on the giving end. Our recent gifts have made us forget our indebtedness. In 1941 the Rockefeller Foundation rendered a wholesome service by including in its report the following: "An American soldier wounded on a battlefield in the Far East owes his life to the Japanese scientist, Kiasoto, who isolated the bacillus of tetanus. A Russian soldier saved by a blood transfusion is indebted to Landsteiner, an Austrian. A German is shielded from typhoid fever with the help of a Russian, Metchnikoff. A Dutch marine in the East Indies is protected from malaria because of the experiments of an Italian, Grassi; while a British aviator in North Africa escapes death from a surgical infection because a Frenchman, Pasteur, and a German, Koch, elaborated a new technique. . . . Our children are guarded from diphtheria by what a Japanese and a German did; they are protected from smallpox by an Englishman's work; they are saved from rabies because of a Frenchman; they are cured of pellagra through the researches of an Austrian. From birth to death they are surrounded by an invisible host—the spirits of men who never thought in terms of flags or boundary lines and who never served a lesser loyalty than the welfare of mankind."

Love of country is one of our noblest emotions and devoutly to be cultivated. But as Edith Cavell, the British nurse, said as she was being led to execution by the Germans for a humanitarian act in Belgium, "Patriotism is not enough." Loyalty to country must be viewed in the light of God's love and in relationship to his whole family, both friends and foes.

Where Does Peacemaking Begin?

When we bring our enmities into the light of God's love, he does not leave us merely looking at them. He calls us to do something about them. This is the clinching formula in Jesus' prescription for loving enemies. He advocated some surprise actions to break the stalemate of hostility. "But if any one strikes you on the right cheek, turn to him the other also."[1] This is a figurative expression suggesting a way of taking an enemy by surprise when he is counting on the continuance of the traditional tit for tat of "An eye for an eye and a tooth for a tooth."[2] To develop love for enemies requires creative, imaginative, ingenious good will.

Here, of course, we must distinguish between peacemaking in personal relationships and on a national scale. But if governments spent one half the money and inventiveness in cultivating world co-operation that they now spend on destructive weapons, I believe they could build brotherhood. Esther Forbes in her *Paul Revere and the World He Lived In* reports that after the battle of Yorktown the American soldiers were left idle. They grew restless and then rebellious. It was then that the word "soldiering" came into our American vocabulary as a term of reproach. Consider the difference in connotation of the word "soldier" in wartime and the word "soldiering" as applied to civilian work in peacetime. The former suggests sacrifice, heroism, service; the latter suggests almost the opposite—killing time,

---

[1] Matthew 5:39.
[2] Matthew 5:38.

lack of interest. Would we not be putting our finger on one of our sorest social spots if we were to say that we Americans have been sufficiently good soldiers to win our wars and then we have "soldiered" in the work of peace? While the churches in their general conventions and assemblies make vigorous statesmanlike pronouncements on world peace, the local parishes are largely uninformed and lukewarm.

To be sure, it is not easy to make peace tasks as challenging as war efforts. In time of war we seem to have the organizing genius to make every individual feel that he or she can do something that counts. But when the war is over and people are asked to help prevent the next one, many say, "It is so complex and nebulous. What can one person do about it?" And often they do nothing. Certainly the organizing genius which can bring war tasks home to the individual can also personalize peace efforts.

But to do so will require an application of skill and ingenuity, a heroism of co-operation and sacrifice comparable to that which men manifest in making war. And is this not the truth which Jesus was driving home when he said: "Do not think that I have come to bring peace on earth; I have not come to bring peace, but a sword"?[3] Christ calls us to fight for fellowship with an intensity never yet approached by our people.

Hear a German who suffered through the Nazification of his own land and wrote before the fires of battle were extinguished: "True peace postulates courage of a higher order than that which war demands; it is a product of spiritual travail and spiritual strength. It is attained when we learn to extinguish the red fires within us and to free our hearts from hate and its destructive power."[4]

To develop such courage of spirit and freedom from hate requires both divine help and daily practice. The home is the magic circle where the egocentric drives of the infant are channeled into the currents of group thinking and living. The range of these currents can and should be enlarged to include the community, the nation, the family of nations. Preparation for world brotherhood is made at

---

[3] Matthew 10:34.
[4] Ernst Juenger, *Peace* (Hinsdale, Ill., 1948), p. 76.

the dinner tables of families as truly as at the conference tables of diplomats. In the home the minds of youth can be conditioned for wholesome race relations. Also the news of the world which can now be brought to the fireside by the radio and television furnishes material for family conversation which should enlarge the understanding and enlighten "the eyes of the heart," to use St. Paul's phrase. Through the lens of the family the best view of human situations is to be obtained. And it is this personalizing of perspective which is so sorely needed.

In developing love for enemies it is high time to heed the old proverb, "The eyes of a fool are on the ends of the earth."[5] The mention of world peace and brotherhood sends our minds off to faraway problems in Moscow or Peking or a race riot in some distant Southern city. Shooting at distant targets and absentee sinners is a favorite sport of preachers as well as politicians. "The longest journey begins with the first step"; so runs an ancient Chinese saying. The road to world peace starts in the minds of men and must be laid from the local communities outward, for, as Chesterton said, nothing is vital until it becomes local. By learning to keep our word as man to man we pave the way and strengthen the faith for the keeping of treaties between nations. By cultivating brotherly relations with other races and groups in our own neighborhood, we gain confidence and skill in the furtherance of global brotherhood. We must guard against insulating our international efforts from the local community just as carefully as we should guard against isolating our local thinking from the world community.

Conferences help to beget mutual understanding if they can be kept from deteriorating into controversy, wherein each party seeks less to find out what is right than to show that he is right. Persons of different races can think and talk together until they achieve such mutual respect that the matter of race is forgotten. *There is too much discussion of interracial problems and not enough interracial discussion of other problems.* When we talk about race issues we focus our minds on racial differences; when we talk together as races about other issues, we forget our differences of color. In the Central

[5] Proverbs 17:24.

Committee of the World Council of Churches, where nationals of South India and Africa shared thoughts freely for several days with members from Scandinavia, Germany, England, America, and other countries, at least one delegate found himself becoming utterly unobservant of color differences. Biology has shown that God hath made of one blood all nations of men. In the laboratory the blood of all races is identical. And the theological discussion of the World Council of Churches demonstrated the kinship and equality of mind under all colors of skin.

As these words are being written world disarmament conferences are at a stalemate and a summit conference is still in question. If it be useless at the moment to meet with the political dictators of Russia, why not try some conferences between scientists and physicians and religious leaders? Public opinion has its power even under dictators. God is at work on both sides of the Iron Curtain and if we are "workers together with God," we can find some channels through the barriers.

Conference without controversy, help without hurting, co-operation without condescension—these are essential factors in supplanting hate and fear with love and hope. Good will cannot flow like a stream from a level which feels itself higher to a level thought of as lower. It must move as the tide moves across the sea—that is, on the level drawn by the attraction of a Power above. It takes God's help to turn enemies into friends.

In the Central Union Church at Honolulu the apse carries these words: "Love never faileth."[6] Standing on an island which has achieved an amazingly peaceful coexistence of races, those words are a symbol of hope as they point toward the now less than peaceful Pacific.

---

[6] 1 Corinthians 13:8 (King James Version).

Why "Peaceful Coexistence" Is Suspect

The expression "peaceful coexistence" is today suspect in many quarters. The crowd thinks of it in terms of our relations with the Russians and fears the pernicious planning and preparations which will go on behind the Iron Curtain while the free world preserves a truce. Peaceful coexistence can never be better than a cold war unless the situation is pervaded by mutual trust begotten by love of God and love of neighbor.

Worthy efforts are being made to patch our broken world. The United Nations, regional associations like NATO and SEATO, and disarmament conferences are among the significant methods by which governmental leaders are seeking to keep the cold war from breaking into flame. More recently it has been suggested that the free world must be prepared to fight some little wars to prevent being forced into a global struggle. The prospect is so ominous that backbreaking military budgets continue but without any cloud-breaking hope.

And now the launching of "sputniks" has opened the thrilling but frightening possibilities of space travel and rendered obsolete many of the protective methods in which we have put our trust.

More and more thoughtful men are realizing that some breaks call for more than patching. This simple but profound truth was put in a nursery jingle which has reason as well as rhyme and needs restudy:

> *Humpty Dumpty sat on a wall,*
> *Humpty Dumpty had a great fall,*
> *All the King's horses and all the King's men*
> *Couldn't put Humpty Dumpty together again.*

When Humpty Dumpty, the egg, is broken, horses and men cannot make it whole again. A new egg has to be laid.

This truth was basic in Jesus' teaching. He was once asked about the Pharisees who were running the official religious system of Palestine and had allowed it to fall into corruption and division. Could not Jesus patch up the Pharisees' system and make it work? No, he said. He explained: "No one sews a piece of unshrunk cloth on an old garment; if he does, the patch tears away from it, the new from the old, and a worse tear is made."[1]

And then Jesus applied this principle to personality when one of the Pharisees, Nicodemus by name, came to interview him. Nicodemus recognized the power of Jesus and hoped that the new Teacher might show him and his fellow Pharisees how they could improve their methods. But Jesus told him bluntly, "You must be born again." He said, ". . . unless one is born anew, he cannot see the kingdom of God."[2] Just as an egg cannot be patched, so in the life of an individual or a group or a system, there come times when a new spirit must be born.

Again, near the end of his earthly ministry, Jesus looked ahead to the company which he foresaw would be recruited by his disciples. Would they become broken into divisions? What could hold them together? And he offered this prayer for his followers: ". . . that they may all be one; even as thou, Father, art in me, and I in thee, that they also may be in us."[3]

Why Christian Coexistence Gives More Promise

Note first that this unifying spirit stems from God. Jesus said, ". . . as thou, Father, art in me, and I in thee, that they also may be in us."

THAN NATIONALISM   Men have tried to generate the spirit of unity by various human methods. When Jesus was born, Augustus Caesar was desperately trying to restore the crumbling foundations of Roman society, which had been undermined by a vast slave population, by economic exploitation, mounting divorce rates, and other

---

[1] Mark 2:21.
[2] John 3:3.
[3] John 17:21.

evils. Caesar enlisted the aid of the popular poet Virgil to help unify the Roman people by recounting the glories of Rome's past and reviving the national pride and spirit. Despite all such efforts, Roman society kept on crumbling.

Although nationalism proved unable to unite the world in the time of Christ and the Caesars, nations are still obsessed with it. Even after the bloody fiascoes of Mussolini and Hitler, the cultivation of national pride is so rife that nationalism has been called man's other religion. By stimulating national pride, it does provide a rallying center within the borders of a country but it erects barriers to world brotherhood. Nationalism is not enough.

THAN MARXISM About a century ago Karl Marx tried another principle for uniting the earth's masses of population. Marx evolved his theories against the background of England's Industrial Revolution. The rapid industrialization and crowding of people into factory towns begot abysmal conditions of poverty and cruelty. Marx came to the conclusion that the only hope of cure was in arousing the workers to unite against the owners. He sought to establish an economic collectivism, now known as communism.

But the motivating principles of Marx's movement were fear and hatred. And while fear and hatred may fuse men for a time into parties or groups, they provide no lasting principle of unity. Witness the bloody purge trials and the recent Kremlin conflicts in the Soviet Union. And we must now beware lest in our efforts to counteract the dangers of communism we resort to methods based on fear and hatred. Such methods are a return to the outworn principle of a balance of powers, or rather a balance of terrors, and lead the nations on in the mad race of armaments toward bankruptcy and future war.

THAN DEMOCRACY A third principle for securing social unity has been that of democracy. It is based on confidence in man's innate goodness and his ability to live peaceably if given freedom to govern himself. But Anatole France, speaking of the extravagant expectations of liberty, equality, and fraternity during the French Revolution, said, "If you begin by thinking that men are naturally good, you will end by wanting to kill them all." Rousseau's theory of restoring paradise by removing the chains of regulation has not proven its validity. The seeds of original sin have sprouted like weeds in fallow ground. Men are prone to use liberty as freedom *from* rather than freedom *for*. Liberty so easily deteriorates into license and irresponsibility.

Why the Unity of the Spirit Is More Than the Spirit of Unity The Judaeo-Christian tradition takes no sentimental view of man's goodness. The Bible portrays man as errant, selfish, sin-ridden, needing to be redeemed. Jesus beheld men from the shadow of the cross, and there can be no more realistic view than that. But seeing men at their worst, Jesus still banked on their best. He said, ". . . and I, when I am lifted up from the earth, will draw all men to myself."[1] Down under the rusted exterior of men, under the rotten surfaces of society, is a core of goodness on which Christ counted as being redeemable by God's love.

While the Christian faith believes in democracy as its principle of human governing, it recognizes that a "government of the people, by the people, for the people," must be a "nation under God." No unity will be achieved and secured merely by men saying, "Let us get together and form a more perfect union, establish justice, insure domestic tranquility, provide for the common defense, promote the general welfare and secure the blessings of liberty to ourselves and our posterity." The framers of America's government realized that men do not rally permanently about a person or an objective unless they believe them to be more than their own creation. People may make an idol of a Hitler or a Mussolini or a Stalin or any other leader but sooner or later they see through the make-up by which such an idol was created, and their devotion disappears.

Christianity posits a divine principle in democracy. Christ is a leader whom men did not set up or elect. Men put Christ on the cross; it was God who set him on a throne. Human beings tried to still his voice by putting him to death, but he would not down. The popularity of Jesus Christ has not been maintained by the efficient propaganda of the Christian church. He has survived the blunders of

---

[1] John 12:32.

the church and the sins of his followers. As a Chinese Christian student put it, "Christ is always being crucified but he does not die." He lighted a faith which the gusty centuries cannot put out, because it is fueled from a divine source.

Christ offers a principle of peaceful coexistence more promising than the narrow loyalties of nationalism or the class hatred of communism or the sentimental optimism of humanistic democracy. The source of Christian unity is in God. ". . . as thou, Father, art in me, and I in thee, that they also may be in us."[2]

Perhaps this deeper principle of unity may be made a bit clearer by a homely illustration. Suppose a group of persons meet at a church on Sunday. They go out to dinner together. Finding themselves congenial, they decide to repeat the practice next Sunday. They keep on doing it. Thus they develop a spirit of unity. But also at church on Sunday is a family. The members go home to dinner. They may not all feel so congenial at the moment. The children may be teasing each other and father may be out of sorts. Nevertheless, theirs is a unity made of God and not of men. They were born into it through the family. And that family unity is stronger than the spirit of unity developed in the group which merely dines together. Let one member of the family be criticized or attacked and all the members rally to him. Let one member of the luncheon group fall under social criticism and he is likely to be dropped.

There is in a family a unity born of God which is normally stronger than any spirit of unity generated by promotion and fellowship. And it is this God-given unity which Christ had in mind for his followers. It is also what St. Paul was thinking about when he urged the Ephesians "to maintain the unity of the Spirit in the bond of peace."[3] The "unity of the Spirit" is something far stronger than a man-made spirit of unity.

This unity of the Spirit is being recognized and demonstrated by the Christian church in its ecumenical gatherings and pronouncements. The divisiveness of the church has been a scandal. But in the World Council of Churches (representing some 170 denomina-

---

[2] John 17:21.
[3] Ephesians 4:3.

tions in 50 countries) there is a profound feeling of unity shared
by the members because they feel themselves bound together by a
common dependence on Christ. Repeatedly this feeling of unity is
voiced even by those who cannot yet bring themselves to share in
the common celebration of the Lord's Supper. Frankly and humbly
members confess that the differences which keep them apart are due
to man's interpretations of Christ and not to Christ himself. Again
and again they repeat St. Paul's rhetorical question, "Is Christ divided?"[4]

Bishop Bergrav of Norway, whose courage and wisdom have made
him a recognized leader of the ecumenical movement, gave one of
the significant addresses at the Evanston meeting of the World
Council of Churches in 1954. He said: "Our unity in Christ, if taken
seriously, prevents us from self-aggrandizement and the feeling of
having a monopoly on all truth, or of being entitled to be the judges
of our fellow churches, rather than being their brethren in Christ.
There exists no master church above the others. What we have got
is a church family in Christ. So I think we may say that the unity in
Christ has started changing the world's church atmosphere."[5]

And we might go on to say that in the realm of atmosphere there
can be maintained no separation of church and state. When the
Protestant ecclesiastical groups begin to feel their unity in the family
of God, the effect will be felt by the governments of the United
States, the United Kingdom, West Germany, and others where Protestantism is potent. And Christlike coexistence within the church
demonstrates at least two principles which can hardly be limited to
Protestantism or even to the church.

How Unity Is Enriched by Diversity

One of these principles is that the quality of the unified group is enriched by the very differences of the elements embraced. Observe
how a growing family is enriched by the diversities of type in the
children. First may come a little girl, sparkling, fun-loving, so sensitive to situations that her laughter may quickly melt into tears. Then

---

[4] 1 Corinthians 1:13.
[5] Proceedings of World Council of Churches, Evanston, 1954.

comes a brother, sober, reserved, quietly thinking things through, never moving until he is convinced and sometimes hard to convince. Then a third child comes along, a little sister with a marked independence of spirit, determined not to be babied or limited because she is the smallest. Each personality makes its contribution to the life and love of the group.

Nowhere is the enrichment of life through differences better seen than in the realm of religion. Think of the diverse types which Jesus took into his original group of disciples. It might almost seem that Jesus purposefully selected his disciples with differences which served as a cross section of humanity.

And in the contemporary church the differences of interpretation and ritual may be viewed in a way that serves to enlarge the dimensions of our faith. For example, in celebrating Holy Communion, as Dr. Cecil Northcutt reminds us, there are some Christians who receive the sacramental elements in a standing position, thus symbolizing the majesty of God, in whose presence they stand at attention. Others there are who receive the sacramental bread and wine sitting at a table, this position suggesting the friendly hospitality of the omnipotent God. The communicants are guests at his table. And then there are other Christians who kneel to receive the bread and wine in an attitude of humility before God, the God who dwells with those "who are of a humble and contrite heart."

Three different attitudes—standing to salute the majesty of God, sitting to share the fellowship of God, kneeling in humility before the infinite compassion of God. These differences in observance serve to enlarge and enrich our conception and experience of God.

We talk so much about tolerating differences within groups. Why not appreciate the possibility of capitalizing them? The community which tries to preserve "a hundred per cent pure Americanism" by keeping out all national and racial groups other than those already dominant in it is forgetting history and forfeiting its future. We owe the strength and richness of the American union to the blending of cultures and colors. The Christians who seek to maintain the strength and purity of their faith by splitting off to form new groups whenever differences appear in the old are depriving themselves of the fullness and richness of life in Christ. Blighting indeed is the narrowing of outlook and sympathy developed in little splinter religious groups and sects. There are some signs that churches and nations are awaking to the truth that freedom and fullness of life and thought are found through unity, which capitalizes differences, rather than through separation, which seeks to escape them. But the awakening must be speeded.

The Divine Principle of At-one-ment

The other principle inherent in Christian coexistence which gives promise of breaking the present world stalemate is that Christ would unite men by the divine principle of self-giving rather than self-defense. God gave himself, "For God so loved the world that he gave his only Son, that whoever believes in him should not perish but have eternal life."[1] And Christ on his part gave himself to God, declaring, "I seek not my own will but the will of him who sent me."[2] The at-one-ment of the Father and the Son was through mutual self-giving. And that is the principle of union which Christ envisages for his followers. ". . . as thou, Father, art in me, and I in thee, that they also may be in us."[3]

In our contemporary world situation both the churches and the states are concerned more with security than with salvation. This is revealed in the sermons of the pulpit. In the effort to make it popular the Christian faith is being presented as security from the threat of communism and other evils which may befall us rather than as salvation from our own sins. Our American government, in order to secure public support, presents its foreign aid program as "enlightened self-interest." While the arguments are valid, they do not constitute the essence of Christ's gospel. Christian peacemaking is more than pacifying and policing. The Beatitudes proclaim the blessedness of the peacemakers, not the peace keepers.[4]

To advance from "peaceful coexistence" to Christian coexistence is the call of Christ and the hope of the world.

The present global alignment between communist and "Christian"

---

[1] John 3:16.
[2] John 5:30.
[3] John 17:21.
[4] Matthew 5:9.

countries, though fraught with immeasurable peril, may prove an unprecedented opportunity for the Christian faith by demonstrating before a world-wide audience that the cross has a redemptive power not possessed by the Kremlin.

And if the followers of Christ do show that they are one, even as God is in Christ and Christ in God, they will hasten the answer to the last clause in Jesus' prayer, "that the world may believe that thou hast sent me."[5]

---

[5] John 17:21.

12 A NEW COMMANDMENT

A New Degree of Love
A New Dimension of Love
A New Dynamic of Love

After Judas had left Our Lord's Last Supper, Jesus turned to his disciples and said, "A new commandment I give to you, that you love one another."[1] In view of all that Jesus had said throughout his ministry about the necessity of loving our fellow men, why did he call this a new commandment?

If he had stopped with the words as quoted above, the command would not have been new. But Jesus added another clause: "even as I have loved you, that you also love one another." In this conditioning clause lies the newness of this commandment.

A New Degree of Love

When Jesus cited his affection for his followers as the yardstick, he gave a *new degree* for measuring love. Think how comparatively pale by contrast would Jesus' words have sounded if in that situation he had repeated the words which he spoke to the inquiring lawyer: "You shall love your neighbor as yourself." The depth of feeling at that Last Supper called for something more than Good Samaritanism. Judas had left the room to arrange the betrayal. Death was impending within a few hours. What could hold the leaderless group together? What could keep them from bitter revenge against the offending disciple and also from recrimination among themselves? Suppose Jesus had merely said: "Whatever you wish that men would do to you, do so to them, for this is the law and the prophets.[1] This is the way I have treated you. I have loved you as I have loved myself. I have had the same regard for your rights and your welfare

---

[1] John 13:34.
[1] Cf. Matthew 7:12.

that I have had for my own. I have practiced the Golden Rule toward you. Now go and apply it to one another."

Lofty as such words might sound from the lips of a Socrates drinking the hemlock; generous as was their sentiment when expressed in parallel form by the great rabbi Hillel, they come far short of the love voiced by Jesus in the Upper Room and lived by him all the way from Nazareth to Calvary. The Golden Rule, noble as it is, uses self-regard or self-respect as the measuring rod of love for others, but Jesus did not gauge his love by what he would want done to himself. His words, "even as I have loved you," express a love utterly selfless, free from all calculation of reciprocity.

The new degree of love demonstrated by Jesus was self-sacrificing to the point where it was "a stumbling-block to Jews."[2] Jewish prophecy proclaimed a Messiah whose wisdom and justice and love almost bankrupted their language to describe: ". . . the government will be upon his shoulder, and his name will be called Wonderful Counselor, Mighty God, Everlasting Father, Prince of Peace."[3] On one high peak of prophetic insight, through eyes washed clear by the tears of exile, a writer did glimpse a Deliverer, "wounded for our transgressions" and "bruised for our iniquities."[4] But the general view of the Jewish people never accepted vicarious suffering as the mark of messiahship and therefore they rejected the gospel of a Christ whose love led him to a cross.

And the selfless love of Jesus was "folly to Gentiles," as well as "a stumbling-block to Jews."[5] The Greek was taught by his Stoic teachers to keep his love within his own control. For example, he was not to love his child too much and then he would not be thrown off balance by its death, not to lose his heart to his wife and then he would not be distraught by her infidelity. "Emotionlessness" or "apathy" was a cultivated ideal.

Such teaching was too cold and loveless for Jesus. He bade men not to hold themselves in to avoid being hurt, but to let themselves

[2] 1 Corinthians 1:23.
[3] Isaiah 9:6.
[4] Isaiah 53:5.
[5] 1 Corinthians 1:23.

out in love beyond bounds of class or nation or race, exposing themselves as love always does to the risk of being hurt.

What folly Jesus' concern for little children must have seemed to
Epictetus, one of the noblest of the Stoics, who asked, how can one
who has to teach mankind go "looking for something to heat the
water in for the baby's bath?"[6] Jesus, with a world mission on his
hands, had time for the littlest and the weakest.

And when we contrast Christ's love with the teaching of Hinduism,
we see what a new note he struck. The central ideal of the Hindu is
holiness. And holiness to the Hindu is a self-absorbed guarding of
one's personality from evil, not an eager, adventurous, self-sacrificing
loving of others. Blamelessness, freedom from taint, is too negative
a virtue to satisfy Christ. "By this all men will know that you are
my disciples, if you have love for one another"—"even as I have
loved you."[7]

A New Dimension of Love

Christ's commandment gives not only a new degree but a *new dimension* of love. His love was more than that of a man sacrificing his
life for his friends. "Greater love has no man than this, that a man
lay down his life for his friends."[1] Yet Jesus gave his life for his
enemies as well as his friends. He was more than a comrade nobly
sacrificing himself to save his company from persecution and death.

Jesus was more than a patriot dying for his country. Not to free
Israel from bondage to Rome did Jesus go to the cross. He gave himself that "whoever believes in him should . . . have eternal life."[2]

And there was a dimension in Jesus' love deeper and tenderer
than that of a martyr sacrificing himself for a cause. A scientist may
so forget himself in the pursuit of truth that he forfeits his life; a
physician may so relentlessly seek the cure of a disease that he becomes infected with the fatal germ; a messenger of the church may
be so determined to extend its outposts that he is put to death by
the devotees of another faith; and yet in all this self-sacrifice a per-

---

[6] Epictetus, Diatr. 3:22.
[7] John 13:34-35.
[1] John 15:13.
[2] John 3:16.

son may lack the personalized love that was in Christ. Paul discerned this and declared, "If I give away all I have, and if I deliver my body to be burned, but have not love, I gain nothing."[3]

When Jesus told the inquiring lawyer that the first commandment was to love God with all the heart and soul and mind and strength and that the second commandment was to love one's neighbor as oneself, the lawyer then asked, "Who is my neighbor?" Apparently the lawyer wished to know how large is the range of this required neighborly love. For answer Jesus told the story of the Good Samaritan, who picked up a wounded man by the roadside, carried him to an inn, and made provision for his future care. Before the Samaritan had come along the Jericho road, a priest and a Levite had passed by, noticed the man who had been robbed and hurt, yet rendered no aid. When Jesus had told the story, he asked the lawyer, "Which of these three, do you think, proved neighbor to the man who fell among robbers?" The lawyer's answer was prompt and obvious: "The one who showed mercy on him."

Jesus was really answering a question different from the one asked by the lawyer. Instead of telling the inquirer to whom he should be neighborly, Jesus defined what it is to be neighborly. A neighbor is one who sees and responds to need. And by choosing as the hero of the story a Samaritan, who to the Jews was a foreigner and outcast, Jesus made it clear that the command to love one's neighbor transcends the bounds of race and nation, of class and creed.

The breadth of Christ's love is a dimension almost beyond our comprehension. The minimum requirement of a decent human being is that he should love those who love him. Yet when we rummage among our recollections, we discover how many channels of reciprocating love we have allowed to dry up even in our more intimate circles. Every Christmas we receive greetings from friends we had almost forgotten.

And from this minimum requisite Christ would have our love reach out to neighbors across the street, across the railroad tracks, across the ocean, across racial lines and iron curtains—all this seems

---

[3] 1 Corinthians 13:3.

a counsel of perfection which "practical Christians" allow to dissolve into a dreamy ideal.

When the Nobile Expedition made its ill-fated attempt to reach the North Pole during the 1920s, the report came back by way of Leningrad that two members of the crew had allowed a comrade to die in the snow because he could not keep up the trek after the dirigible had been wrecked. The Russians raised a cry over the inhumanity of allowing a man to perish in such a situation. But about that time an American church was distributing food supplies to some famine-stricken areas of Russia. One of the Soviet officials sternly asked the representatives of the church what hidden motive brought them over to that land, what ax the Americans were trying to grind. It was one thing to understand why you should not let a man freeze in the snow at your feet; it was quite another to understand why you would come halfway around the world to feed the starving. This missionary dimension of Christ's love is beyond the comprehension of the non-Christian—in fact it is beyond the understanding of many who sit in church pews.

After the First World War, in the exuberant expectation of the new day of brotherhood which was to follow, A. S. M. Hutchinson wrote a best seller under the title, *If Winter Comes*. The central figure felt the call to be a Good Samaritan to an outcast and incurred social ostracism for his efforts. He couched his motivation in these words: "Here was a human creature come to us . . . breathing the same air, sharing the same mortality, responsible to the same God. If you've got a grain, a jot of humanity, you must out of the very flesh and bone of you respond to the cry of one made as you yourself are made."

To respond to the needs of a human being just because he is a human being—such is the breadth of Christ's love. But society has not yet had the "power to comprehend with all the saints what is the breadth and length and height and depth, and to know the love of Christ which surpasses knowledge."[4]

And Christ demonstrated a *length* of *love* quite as new as his dimension of breadth. A constant note in his ethical theory is the ex-

---

[4] Ephesians 3:18–19.

travagant length to which love must go. "If any one forces you to go one mile, go with him two miles."[5] The hated Roman soldiers who patrolled Palestine could require a Jew to carry their equipment a mile. Such a demand was galling, but Jesus bade his followers go even beyond the line of duty.

"If any one strikes you on the right cheek, turn to him the other also."[6] This figure of speech was an arresting way of commanding his disciples to return good for evil. To strike back would be what the assailant expected; to turn the other cheek would at least arrest his attention if not his fist. It might break the chain reaction of retaliation. It might even break the bitter heart of the wrongdoer, as did the bishop's generous act when he handed the other candlestick to Jean Valjean, the ex-convict.

"Then Peter came up and said to him, 'Lord, how often shall my brother sin against me, and I forgive him? As many as seven times?' Jesus said to him, 'I do not say to you seven times, but seventy times seven.'"[7]

Such counsels seem extravagant to the point of unreality. We so often lack the patience and perseverance to preserve our friendships. In our charities we frequently fail to follow through our contributions to make them effective. In fact we sometimes give mainly to get rid of the request or to keep our social standing. The roads of life are strewn with the wreckage of run-down and half-finished loves.

The lengths to which we go in our love determine the value of its breadth. A popular speaker in the enthusiasm of his eloquence recently exclaimed, "I love everybody." The expansiveness of his emotion was due to the emptiness of his thought. At least one listener knew of a few specific spots where his love was pretty sterile. He had not gone to the length of thinking in concrete situations. Others think themselves broad-minded largely because they lack deep convictions. Much indifference masquerades as tolerance.

To what lengths do we go to find out the facts, to give the benefit of the doubt, to forgive the unforgiving? We often take comfort and

---

[5] Matthew 5:41.
[6] Matthew 5:39.
[7] Matthew 18:21–22.

pride in appraising our improved ministries of healing and philanthropy as marks of our increasing brotherly love. We think how "good samaritanism" has grown into organized charities, community chests, and the Red Cross. And truly it does hearten us to see the progress being made in the methods of helpfulness, even amid the mounting piles of destructive weapons. But all this still leaves us far behind the creative spirit of Christ's love.

To go out of our way to find those in need, to go forth and seek the sinner and those who feel sunk, to knock on the doors of those too shy or too proud to ask for help—that is the compassion which Christ taught and lived.

And often the persons most worth helping are those who do not ask for assistance, those who suffer silently, or perhaps those who do not know their own needs. A man is not always aware of what he really needs. He knows when he has lost his money or his health; he does not always know when he has lost his vision or his lovableness. A true friend or neighbor reveals to us our needs as well as responds to them.

A gentleman has been defined as one who never puts his feelings before the rights of others or his rights before their feelings. So far, so good. But Christ calls us to study until we understand the feelings of others and to sacrifice until we help others to secure their rights.

A gentleman is decent enough to obey the commandment, "Honor your father and your mother." But Christ filled family love with such tender concern and true fidelity that parents and children are worthy of love.

A gentleman obeys the commandment, "You shall not kill." But Christ went beyond that to serve and sacrifice in order to save and enrich life.

A gentleman keeps the commandment, "You shall not commit adultery." But Christ gave a new social standing to womanhood which ennobles the marriage bond.

A gentleman observes the commandment, "You shall not steal." But Christians are called not only to respect property rights but also to "bear one another's burdens, and so fulfil the law of Christ."[8]

---

[8] Galatians 6:2.

A gentleman adheres to the commandment, "You shall not bear false witness against your neighbor." But Christ said to his followers, ". . . you will know the truth, and the truth will make you free"[9] —free from prejudice and suspicion and blinding hate.

A gentleman obeys the tenth commandment, "You shall not covet your neighbor's house or your neighbor's wife . . . or anything that is your neighbor's." A Christian is not only to refrain from coveting but is also to further his neighbor's welfare.

The Mosaic Code calls men to keep its laws; Christ calls men to keep his love, "even as I have loved you." Law is conforming, love is creative and transforming. Christlike love sets no limits to which it will go: "Love bears all things, believes all things, hopes all things, endures all things. Love never ends."[1]

A New Dynamic of Love

But does not this new and infinite dimension of Christlike love drive our finite minds to despair? It is too high. We cannot attain unto it. So it strikes us at first sight. But the testimony of experience is that Christ's new commandment gives a *new dynamic* to human love.

The words, "even as I have loved you," awaken the power of the imagination.

> . . . we're made so that we love
> First when we see them painted, things we have passed
> Perhaps a hundred times nor cared to see.[1]

Christ gave a portrait of divine love so personal that it penetrates where abstractions do not reach. He brought God's love down to the dimensions of the manger, the market place, the sickroom, the empty tomb. He transformed the command to love God from the push of duty to the pull of desire.

We do not hate those whom we believe to love us truly. We may be provoked by the persistence of an affection which asks what we cannot give, but we cannot hate the true love which gives without

---

[9] John 8:32.
[1] 1 Corinthians 13:7–8.
[1] Robert Browning, *Fra Lippo Lippi.*

demanding. Christ's love was so utterly selfless that no man can hate him when once he is understood.

Men do at times hate God. They shake their fists in his face and denounce him for what seems to them his indifference and his injustice. But their bitterness is turned to love if they can be convinced that God is like Christ. And that conviction is what Christ came to bring. He declared, "He who has seen me has seen the Father."[2] He also told his hearers how they could test his claim to speak for God. He said: "My teaching is not mine, but his who sent me; if any man's will is to do his [God's] will, he shall know whether the teaching is from God or whether I am speaking on my own authority."[3]

By demonstrating a limitless love as the incarnation of divine love, Christ prepared a soil in which brotherly love is nurtured. Parental affection is the soil which begets love between members of a family. Horace Dutton Taft has a whimsical and revealing paragraph in his *Memories and Opinions,* which illustrates the ties that bound the brothers together in the famous Taft family. He quotes from a letter on the day of his birth, December 28, 1861, by his father to his maternal grandfather. After telling of Horace's arrival, the father writes: "Willie [the future President of the United States] is very much displeased about it. . . . Louise [the mother] has, however, compromised the matter with him and the baby is to remain a while, and if he does not behave well he is to be sent to the orphan asylum, but if he behaves well we may keep him." Horace Taft adds, "Evidently I behaved well, for I never went to the orphan asylum."[4]

Children in a home may at first resent the coming of new babies to divide the parental care and the nursery playthings. What changes the spirit of competition to that of co-operation among the growing members of the family? It is the love given by father and mother as the soil in which the young lives grow.

Similar in principle is the figure of speech which Paul uses to nourish love among his fellow members in the family of God: ". . . that Christ may dwell in your hearts through faith; that you, being rooted and grounded in love, may have power to comprehend

---

[2] John 14:9.
[3] John 7:16–17.
[4] Horace Dutton Taft, *Memories and Opinions* (New York, 1942), p. 7.

with all the saints what is the breadth and length and height and depth, and to know the love of Christ which surpasses knowledge, that you may be filled with all the fullness of God."[5]

If Christlike love were only a pattern for us to copy, it would be our despair. But Christ is a person with whom we can enter into communion until we feel the contagion of his presence and the lift of his love. Henry George, the American humanitarian, was once talking to Cardinal Manning, the English prelate, of their common interests. "I loved the people," said George, "and that love brought me to Christ as their best friend and teacher." Manning replied, "And I loved Christ and so learned to love the people for whom he died."

While the title of this book, "Man's First Love," is derived from the first and great commandment in the Jewish law, the purport of its pages has been to show that man's love for God is possible only through God's love for man. We can keep his commandment only as we feel his compassion. "We love, because he first loved us."[6]

---

[5] Ephesians 3:17–19.
[6] 1 John 4:19.